TREE PRUNING
A WORLDWIDE PHOTO GUIDE

By

ALEX L. SHIGO

Shigo and Trees, Associates
4 Denbow Road, Durham
New Hampshire, 03824

DEDICATION

To Marilyn and Toby

The Author: Alex L. Shigo was born in Duquesne, Pennsylvania on May 8, 1930. He received his BS in Biology from Waynesburg College in 1956 and his MS and PhD in Plant Pathology from West Virginia University in 1958 and 1959, respectively. From 1959 to 1985 he was employed by the US Forest Service as chief scientist and Project Leader of a Pioneering Project on Discoloration and Decay in Forest Trees. He has dissected over 15,000 trees with a chainsaw. He has studied trees in many countries. His research yielded 270 publications and he has received many honors and awards. He believes that we must help trees by helping the people who work with trees by providing sound educational programs based on research.

Shigo, Alex L., 1930-
  Tree pruning: a worldwide photo guide for the proper pruning of trees / by Alex L. Shigo.
  p. 192 cm.
  Bibliography: p. 181
  Includes index.

  ISBN 0-943563-08-9

  1. Ornamental trees—Pruning.   2. Trees—Pruning.
I. Title.

SB435.76.S53   1989
635.9'77—dc19   88-36722
                                                     CIP

Copyright 1989 by Shigo and Trees, Associates
Durham, New Hampshire 03824   USA

Printed in the United States of America

Cover—Rings of woundwood on the white oak trunk indicate proper pruning.

PREFACE

The aim of this guide is to present results of scientific research on pruning in a way that can be understood easily by all people who care about trees.

A major problem throughout the history of tree pruning has been the scant attention given to pruning as it affects the health of trees, while great attention has been given to pruning as it affects the desires of man.

In this guide I discuss pruning for the desires of man, but also for the health of the trees and their associates.

When a few simple concepts on tree growth are understood, proper pruning becomes simple and a matter of common sense.

I have tried to make this guide easy to read, easy to understand, and easy to put into practice. I hope you find it that way.

I emphasize that this is a guide and not a rule book full of absolutes. Themes are presented. There will always be variations on the themes.

And finally, please use great care and caution when pruning. Because information is given does not mean that laymen should attempt all pruning operations. For help and advice on pruning, consult tree care professionals—arborists.

ACKNOWLEDGEMENTS

I thank the United States Forest Service for supporting my research on trees for 26 years, and for use of some of the photographs in the book.

I thank Kenneth Dudzik, Dr. David Funk, Dr. E. Alan McGinnes, Niels Hvass, Nelson Rogers, Dr. Walter Shortle and Klaus Vollbrecht for help with the pruning studies; and I thank the black walnut veneer-log buyer who told me he would not buy trees that had been flush pruned. I wanted to know why!

I thank the reviewers who gave valuable comments for the improvement of the manuscript: Kenneth Dudzik, Pius Floris, Peter Gerstenberger, John Harmer, Way and Geraldine Hoyt, Sharon Ossenbruggen, Everett Rowley, Marilyn A. Shigo, Dr. Kevin Smith, Klaus Vollbrecht, Bruce Wilhelm, and Dr. Daniele Zanzi.

I thank Klaus Vollbrecht for bringing to my attention the need to clarify the meaning of callus.

CONTENTS

Introduction 1
Pruning problems 9
Safety First 16
Easy answers, difficult actions 17
Branch anatomy 18
Branch shedding 21
Protection zone 22
Branch collars 24
Branch bark ridge (BBR) 26
Natural target pruning 28
Woundwood after pruning 32
Improper cuts 33
Inside view: Proper, improper 35
Flush cuts and problems 40
Dead branch removal 50
Stubs 61
Callus confusion 63
Codominant stems 70
Included bark 78
Tree form 83
Training cuts 94
Topping 98
Pollarding 104
Shaping 110
Espalier 111
Shearing 113
Woody vines 114
Fruit trees 115
Planting 116
Pruning big trees 119
Over pruning 120
Tree hazards 124
Regulating size and shape 126
Wound dressings 128
Root pruning 132
Sprouts 134
Wildlife 135
Bonsai 136
Tree dignity 137
Future 138
Trees and people 139
Trees and their associates 140

APPENDIX

How trees grow and
  defend themselves 141
What keeps you alive will
  eventually kill you 144
History of tree pruning problems 146
Dr. Hans Mayer-Wegelin
  and the history of pruning 148
Dr. Robert Hartig and pruning 150
Branch anatomy 151
Woundwood after proper cut 152
Woundwood after improper cut 153
Branch protection zone 154
Large pruning cuts on old trees 155
Codominant stems 156
Trunk collar 157
Codominant stems
  on American elm 158
Proper pruning of a branch with
  included bark 162
Intermittent included bark 163
Callus and woundwood 164
Cracks, wetwood, and
  branch failure 165
Cladoptosis, tools 166
Cavity treatments 167
Cabling and bracing 168
Shigometry 169
CODIT 170
Tree hazards 172
Proper planting and pruning 174
Pruning and energy 176
Pruning and fertilizing,
  and phenology 177
Postlude 180
References 181
Index 189

And the fox said to the little prince: "Men have forgotten this truth. But you must not forget it. You become responsible, forever, for what you have tamed."

The Little Prince
Antoine de Saint Exupery

1

PROPER PRUNING

Respects Tree Beauty
Respects Tree Defense Systems
Respects Tree Dignity

IMPROPER PRUNING

Destroys Tree Beauty
Destroys Tree Defense Systems
Destroys Tree Dignity

Australia

TREES HAVE GROWN FOR MILLIONS OF YEARS IN FORESTS

Forest trees have long slender trunks.
Lower branches are shed when they are small.
(This is the tallest hardwood in the world; *Eucalyptus regnans*,
over 95 meters tall with a broken top.)

Denmark

WE HAVE BROUGHT TREES INTO OUR WORLD

City trees usually have short robust trunks and large lower branches.
We have changed the way trees grow.
WE are responsible for their proper care.

PROPER CARE

starts with an understanding of how trees grow and defend themselves.

Trees grow taller and bigger, and live longer than any organism ever to inhabit earth. Trees are compartmented, woody, perennial, shedding plants. They usually have a single central trunk. The tree framework is made up of wood.

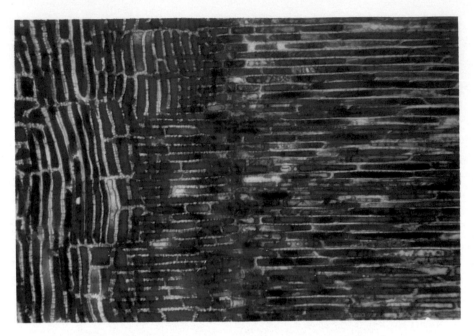

New Hampshire

WOOD IS NOT DEAD!

Wood is a tissue made up of living, dying, and dead cells in a highly ordered arrangement. The cell walls consist of cellulose and lignin.

Sapwood in trunks, branches, and roots have more living cells than dead cells. The living cells are small. The dead fibers and transport cells are large.

Above is a stained section of living cells in wood. Living cells store energy reserves for many tree processes, especially defense.

When pruning removes wood that has living cells, the energy storage system of the tree is affected. When energy storage is affected, growth and defense are affected.

Courtesy, John M. Phillips   California

LIMITS TO TREE DEFENSE

Proper pruning is a beneficial tree practice. But, too often people think that because trees are so big and tough, you can prune them in any way, and treat them in any way and they will continue to defend themselves. We are seeing now that this is not so. There are limits to what a tree will endure.

This oak was over pruned. The cuts destroyed a defense system. There was rot in the branches. Thick coatings of wound dressing protected the rot. Construction activities injured the roots. The tree died. People loved this tree. They wanted to be close to it. They killed it because they did not understand how trees grow. This scene is repeated many times.

TIME FOR SOME CHANGES

For centuries, man has inflicted injuries to trees in the name of pruning.
Now, trees in cities and forests worldwide are in trouble for many reasons.

It is time for some changes in the ways we treat trees. Decisions must be made on the basis of an understanding of tree biology. The information must come from scientific research.

PRUNING BASED ON RESEARCH

Recommendations for centuries have stated how to cut branches *off* trees.
Research on how branches come *on* trees was not published until 1985.

This guide is based on that research, and on related research that I did with the help of many hard-working people over 30 years.

PRUNING PROBLEMS

Changes must be made to 7 tree practices that cause serious injury to trees. The practices all deal with pruning.

Australia

1. WRONG TREE, WRONG PLACE

The tree is later mutilated.

Know what size and shape of tree you want. Little trees grow to become big trees.

Know your planting site.

Select trees that will grow best on your site.

Get advice from professionals.

California

2. FLUSH CUTS

A major tree defense system is destroyed.
Make pruning cuts as close as possible to the collar at the branch base.
Do not injure or remove the collar.

California

3. STUB CUTS

Stubs are food for organisms that start rot and cankers.
Do not leave living or dead stubs.
The swollen branch collar is not a stub.

Florida

4. TOPPING AND TIPPING LARGE TREES

The practice causes serious injuries to large trees and leads to hazardous conditions. Do not plant trees under power lines.

Or, plant only small-maturing species.

Or, start pruning when the trees are small.

Australia

5. OVER PRUNING

The tree framework is destroyed.
The tree becomes a dangerous hazard.
Roots are weakened. Root diseases start.
Excessive sprouting starts.
Boring insects infest the wood.

Italy

6. IMPROPER POLLARDING

Tree mutilation is often called pollarding. Proper pollarding is a fine tree practice. Start with a tree that lends itself to pollarding. Establish the desired framework when the tree is young and small. Remove sprouts every year. Do not injure the pollard heads.

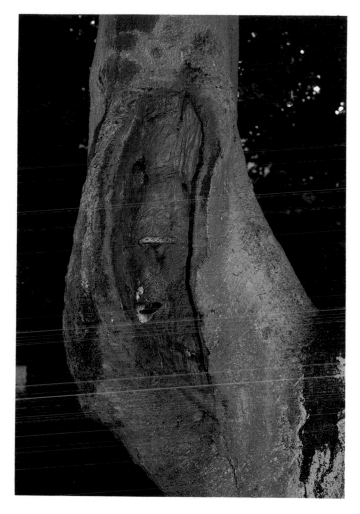

Sweden

7. WOUND DRESSINGS

Wound dressings do not stop rot.

Do not apply dressing over rotted or infected wood.

Some dressings stimulate rot.

Some wound dressings stimulate the growth of woundwood, often incorrectly called callus. The woundwood may roll inward to form a "rams horn" and closure may be prevented.

Before we discuss details of these practices and tree biology, it is important to know some basic rules of safety.

15

SAFETY FIRST

Pruning trees can be fun. It can also be very dangerous.

This guide gives pruning information for tree care professionals — arborists — and laymen, but this does not mean that the laymen should always do the pruning.

Here are some safety rules for laymen:
- If you have to get on a ladder, the tree is too large for you to prune.
- If the branch is over 2 inches in diameter, do not do it.
- Use protective hats, gloves, glasses, and wear a long-sleeved shirt.
- Use sharp tools that are in proper working condition.
- Do not work near power lines!
- Never use a chainsaw.
- Stay away from storm-injured trees.
- Know where your cord is on electric shears.
- Concentrate on your job.
- **Know your limits and the limits of your tools: when in doubt, call a professional.**

Here are some rules professionals know and practice:
- Have proper training before working near power lines.
- Wear safety gear at all times.
- Know where your partners are at all times.
- Respect the power of a chainsaw and use it properly and safely.
- Do not put climbing ropes over weak branches.
- Check all equipment and tools before you get into the tree.
- Do not work when you are tired or alone.
- Do not ignore cuts and bruises.
- Do only what you have been trained to do!
- Report accidents.
- Have regular safety meetings.

Talk and Think Safety.

EASY ANSWERS, DIFFICULT ACTIONS

The answers to proper pruning are very easy and simple. To get people to do the easy and simple procedures is very difficult. Here they are:

Decide what kind of trees you want: tall, small, weeping, fruit bearing, etc.

Learn what kind of site you have: wet, dry, acid, alkaline, clay, sand, etc.

Talk to tree professionals: nurserymen, consulting arborists, extension people and others. They will tell you which trees will give you what you want on your site.

Select the right trees for the right planting site.

Do not plant trees that will grow big: in small spaces, under power lines, or close to buildings.

Do not plant trees that have low branches near walkways or streets.

Do not buy trees that have cankers, wounds, included bark, sunken spots under branches, cracks, flush cuts, poor form, girdling roots, or wound dressings. Do not buy trees that have been in containers so long that roots are spiraling.

Start pruning early in the life of the tree to establish the framework for the kind of tree you want. The framework is the basic woody design of the tree that determines the shape or architecture of the tree. Architecture is the complete structure of the tree.

Keep pruning at regular intervals to maintain the architecture of the tree.

The answers are easy: select the right tree for the right site, start pruning early, and keep it up. To get these three simple actions done is very difficult! Remember, little trees grow up to become big trees, and branches stay at the same position on the trunk.

START PROPER PRUNING EARLY

Proper pruning is the removal of living, dying, and dead parts of trees to benefit trees and their associates and man.

Trees benefit when branches are removed that could result in large wounds if they fell. Proper pruning corrects defective form that could result in branch failure. When a branch falls, it dies.

Man benefits from proper pruning by obtaining higher quality lumber and fruit. Proper pruning gives man the tree architecture wanted for shade, beauty, or windbreaks.

Tree associates benefit by having a place to live for a long time.

We will now start by reviewing how branches grow, die, and shed.

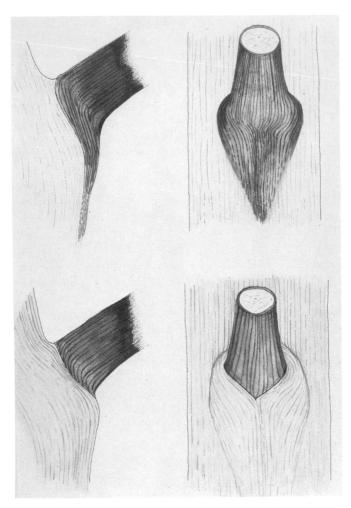

New Hampshire

HOW BRANCHES ARE ATTACHED TO TRUNKS

Branch tissues (red) start growth before trunk tissues.
Branch tissues turn abruptly at the branch base to form a collar.
Trunk Tissues (yellow) grow later and form a trunk collar over the branch collar.

18

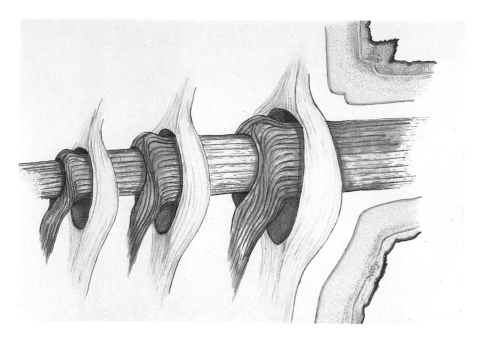

New Hampshire

BRANCH DIAGRAM

Three growth rings are pulled apart in the diagram. Trunk collars (yellow) envelop the branch collars (red). Tissues in the bark follow the same pattern. Water and elements move from root to branch in the red tissues, and from root to tissues above the branch in the yellow tissues.

Photosynthate, or tree food—sugar— moves from leaves on the branch toward the root in the inner bark along a pattern shown in red. Food from leaves and branches above the one shown here move toward the root in the inner bark along a pattern shown in yellow.

New Hampshire

COLLARS ON TREES

Branch collars and trunk collars can be seen when trunks are split as shown here. The trunk collars and branch collars are called collectively the branch collar.

The collar is a place where bark and wood of branch and trunk come together. The collar is like a tissue "switching zone".

New Hampshire

NATURAL SHEDDING OF BRANCHES

As branches die, many organisms grow on the bark and in the branch wood. They seldom grow into the trunk. The branch tissues connect with the trunk tissues by a thin strip of tissues shown in red in the diagram on page 19. After the branch dies, the trunk collar grows over the thin strip of branch tissues below the base of the branch. The organisms on the branch bark then have no connection with trunk bark.

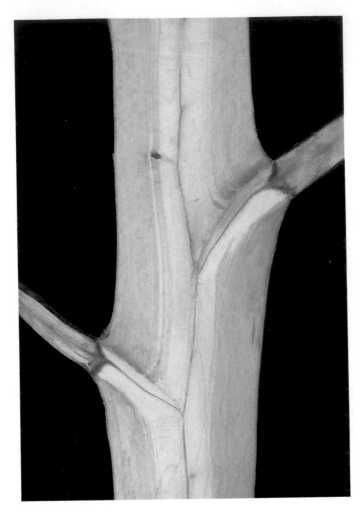

New Hampshire

PROTECTION ZONES

Protection zones form within the bases of branches. The zones are made up of chemicals that come from stored energy reserves — starch, oil — in living wood cells. The zones resist spread of organisms from the branch into the trunk. The chemicals are phenol-based in hardwoods and terpene-based in conifers.

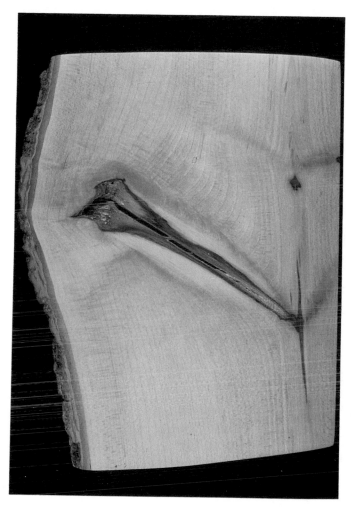

New Hampshire

WALLED OFF BRANCH CORE

When the branch falls, the wood core is walled off in the trunk. Rot seldom spreads into the healthy wood. Trees compartmentalize injured and infected wood. Compartmentalization is a tree defense process where boundaries form that resist spread of pathogens. The boundaries also defend the liquid transport, energy storage, and mechanical support systems of the tree.

Maine

BRANCH COLLARS

Branch collars are rings of wood with living cells about the bases of branches. Great care must be taken not to injure or remove the collars on young and old trees when pruning. All branches on woody plants have branch collars.

DO NOT INJURE OR REMOVE COLLARS

Branch collars on some trees are very large, as shown here. There is great variation in size of the branch collars on the same tree.

The collar that remains after proper pruning is not a branch stub. A proper pruning cut is based on the collar and not on a set angle of cut.

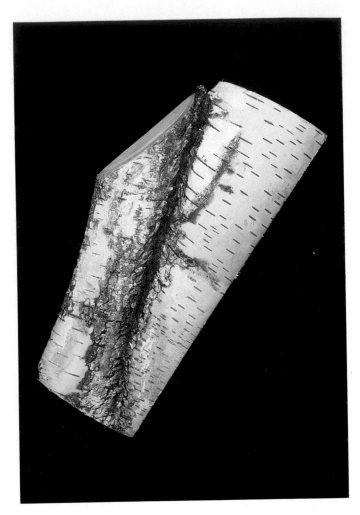

New Hampshire

BRANCH BARK RIDGE

The branch bark ridge (BBR) is raised bark that forms within the branch crotch. It remains on the trunk as the tree grows. The BBR is the black ridge on the white birch. The BBR is the key to proper pruning.

The BBR shows the angle of the branch core in the tree. On some trees—London plane and smooth-barked eucalypts—the BBR is shed with the outer bark. Still, an indentation remains on the trunk where the BBR formed.

Maine

DO NOT PLACE PRUNING TOOLS BEHIND THE BBR

Do not leave branch stubs. Cut along the red line, as shown here.

A cut behind the BBR in the crotch destroys the protection zone within the branch collar.

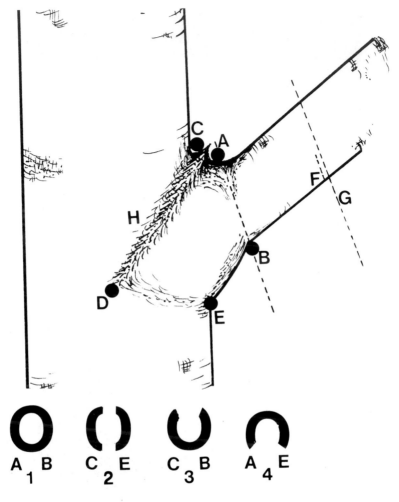

NATURAL TARGET PRUNING

Locate the branch bark ridge (H) and the branch collar (E to B).
Stub cut the branch (up F, down G).
Locate points A and B where the branch meets the branch collar.
Cut from A to B, or from B to A with care.
If position of B is uncertain, draw a line in your mind from A to E.
Angle EAD is approximately the same as angle EAB.
Point D is the beginning of the branch bark ridge (H).
A proper cut will result in woundwood pattern 1.
Improper cuts will result in patterns 2, 3, and 4.
Do not leave stubs.
Do not make flush cuts.
Do not paint the wounds.

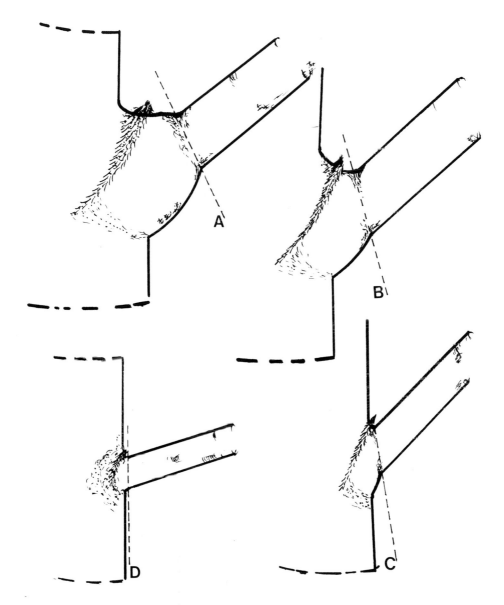

BRANCH COLLARS AND ANGLES OF CUTS

Proper pruning of a living branch is a cut as close as possible to the branch collar. There is no set angle for a proper cut.

Cuts A, B, C, and D are proper cuts.

New Hampshire

FLAT COLLARS

Conifers often have flat branch collars. A straight cut close to the collar is a correct cut. Some trees, such as junipers and cedars, have living branches sunken within the branch collars. A proper cut for such branches is a cut to the base of the collar. The cut should not injure the collar. We have no tools to make such a cut.

New Hampshire

NO SET ANGLE FOR A PROPER CUT

The proper angle of cut will depend on the branch collar. Always stub cut the branch first. Sap may flow when cuts are made before the growing season. The flowing sap is part of the tree's defense system. To avoid sap flow on birches and maples and other similar trees, prune immediately after leaves have matured. The best times to prune most trees are during the late dormant season and immediately after leaves and needles form. If possible, do not prune when leaves are forming or falling. If proper pruning cuts are infected, the pathogens will spread in a small strip of wood below the cut. This is true for Dutch elm disease, oak wilt, and fire blight.

Missouri

WOUNDWOOD RINGS

A ring of woundwood forms about proper cuts. The woundwood forms above and below the cut. Make pruning cuts that result in rings of woundwood.

Callus is undifferentiated tissue with little or no lignin.

Woundwood is highly ordered wood with lignin.

After wounding, some callus forms about the margins of the wound. Then large woody ribs form that begin to close the wound. The woody ribs are woundwood.

Denmark

WOUNDWOOD AND IMPROPER CUTS

Woundwood forms only to the sides of improper cuts. The living tissues above and below the cuts die back. Woundwood usually forms later under the bark. Even minor pruning mistakes made at the time of leaf formation or leaf shedding may result in major injuries to the tree.

South Korea

OVAL-SHAPED WOUNDWOOD

Long oval-shaped woundwood indicates old improper cuts. Rot develops rapidly after improper cuts. Removal of the fungus fruit body will not stop the development of the rot. The greatest diameter of the rot column will be the diameter of the tree at the time the wound was inflicted.

Missouri

INSIDE VIEW OF IMPROPER CUT

Improper cuts remove the branch collar and the branch protection zone, and the cuts wound the trunk.

Trees, during their hundreds of millions of years on this earth, never experienced this type of injury until man came along with pruning tools and a poor understanding of trees.

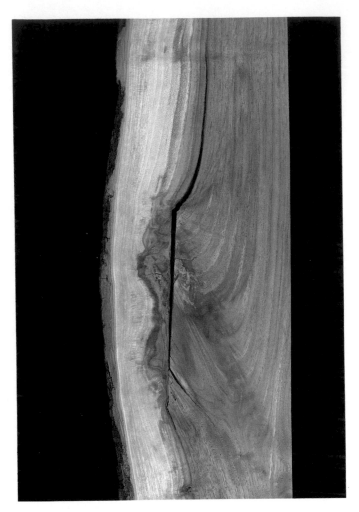

Illinois

IMPROPER CUTS AND PROBLEMS

Wounds made by improper cuts may close, but rot and cracks often develop. Cracks and rot ruin wood for high quality wood products. Cracks and rot weaken the tree and lead to hazardous trees.

Washington

INSIDE VIEW OF PROPER CUT

A proper cut after nine years in a deodar cedar. The colored central core was the diameter of the tree at the time of pruning. The wound closed and compartmentalized the pathogens and no rot or cracks developed. Natural target pruning is effective for large branches and small branches. (Michael Schnad)

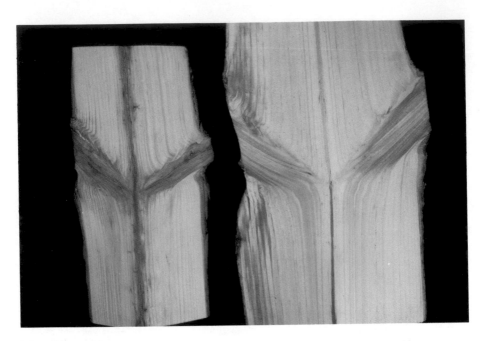

New Hampshire

COMPARISON OF PRUNING CUTS ON PINE

Dissected samples of red pine (left) and white pine (right) one year after each was pruned with an improper cut to the left and a proper cut to the right of each sample. The branch cores of conifers are impregnated with protective resin substances while the branches are alive.

Improper cuts expose trunk wood that has living cells and is not impregnated with protective substances.

Maine

COMPARISON OF PRUNING CUTS ON OAK

Two samples from the same red oak tree that had branches of the same size and age cut off 6 years before the tree was dissected. The improper cut at left had large ribs of woundwood and a large column of rot. No rot developed after the proper cut. A ring of woundwood formed and the wood-inhabiting organisms were compartmentalized.

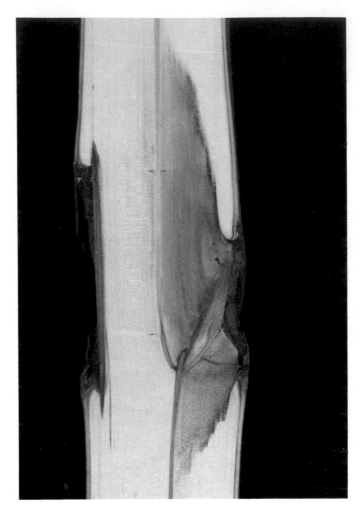

Maine

WHY FLUSH CUTS INJURE TREES

Flush cuts are improper pruning cuts that remove the branch collar and the wood where the branch protection zone forms. Flush cuts expose the trunk wood to infections. The experimentally inflicted trunk wound at left is much larger in area than the flush cut at right. Flush cuts destroy a major tree defense system.

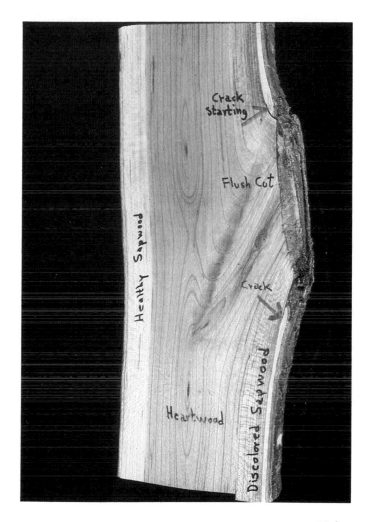

Maine

FLUSH CUTS AND WEAK DEFENSE

One healthy growth ring is above and below the flush cut on the cherry sample. The current growth ring has a weak defense system because it does not store energy reserves until the end of the growth period. Insects and microorganisms often attack the weak growth ring. Sudden changes in temperature may cause the weak growth ring to crack.

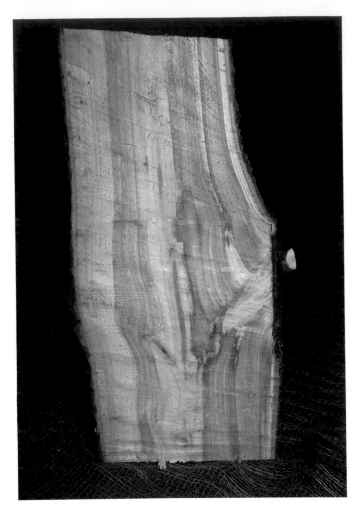

Denmark

FLUSH CUTS AND SAPWOOD REDUCTION

A thin band of healthy sapwood is above and below the 8-year-old flush cut at right on the Norway spruce. A thick band of healthy sapwood is on the left of the sample. Rot is in the wood above and below the flush cut. The discolored and decayed wood above and below the flush cut was the wood present at the time the cut was made. The pathogens did not spread into the wood that formed after the cut was made.

FLUSH CUTS AND INSECT PROBLEMS

Insects often infest the weakened but still living tissues above and below flush cuts. Wounds made by flush cuts and by climbing spikes, especially at the time leaves are forming, often attract insects that carry microorganisms that may cause serious tree diseases—fungi that cause Dutch elm disease and oak wilt. Infections could be reduced greatly by stopping these improper practices. Do not prune elms and oaks during their early growth period.

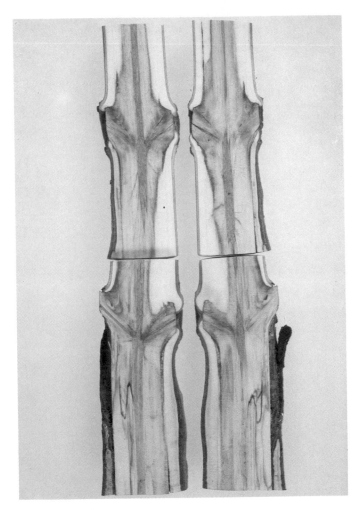

New Hampshire

FLUSH CUTS AND DEAD SPOTS

Dead spots develop on young trees when many flush cuts are inflicted at the same time. Frost and heat are often blamed for the injuries—cracks, dead bark, dead roots.

Trees in nurseries are often grown with many low branches to increase the girth of the trunk. As the time for sale approaches, the lower branches are removed. Many flush cuts in vertical alignment cause serious injury to the tree.

Maine

FLUSH CUTS AND CRACKS

The long crack was started by the flush cut, not the frost.

The flush cuts start internal cracks that split easily when the bark is exposed to sudden heat or cold. The heat and cold are important factors, but they are secondary factors, not initiating factors.

45

California

FLUSH CUTS AND HEAT INJURY

The injured bark was started by the flush cut, not heat. Heat, cold, drought, and other factors may speed the drying, dying, and cracking of tissues weakened by flush cuts.

Florida

FLUSH CUTS AND ROOT PROBLEMS

The sunken spot above and below the flush cut on this live oak is a place where many organisms may attack. The weakened tissues may extend to the roots and lead to root diseases. Some pathogens spread so rapidly in the weakened tissues that they are often thought to be the primary cause of the problem. Species of fungi in the genera *Hypoxylon* and *Nectria* are good examples. They spread rapidly in tissues that are still alive but have a very weak defense system. (Robert Kyle)

Colorado *Courtesy, Dr. James Feucht*

FLUSH CUTS AND CANKERS

Cankers often develop after flush cuts.

Proper pruning of peach trees significantly reduces the occurrence of Cytospora canker. Proper pruning can significantly reduce the occurrence of cankers caused by many other pathogens.

California

FLUSH CUTS AND SPROUTS

Excessive sprouting often develops after flush cuts. Flush cuts on young trees may start sprout burls that persist for the life of the tree.

Flush cuts cause weakened tissues above and below the cut (see page 41). Sprouts form when energy reserves decrease in wood. Sprouts are an emergency system to return energy reserves to the tree. When sprouts form in shaded spots, they do not return energy to the tree. The sprouts die.

Some trees form many sprouts even after proper cuts. To reduce sprouting, make proper cuts after the new leaves have formed.

New Hampshire

DEAD BRANCHES

Cut dead and dying branches as close as possible to the ring of living wood at the branch base. Do not injure living tissues.

Sweden

SCRIBING PRUNING CUTS

Do not scribe living trunk tissues above and below a flush cut. Rot will develop rapidly regardless of other treatments.

When it is necessary to scribe wounds, make scribing cuts as shallow as possible. Do not enlarge the wound. Do not point the vertical tips of the wound. It is not necessary to scribe in the form of a vertical ellipse. Make all margins smooth and rounded.

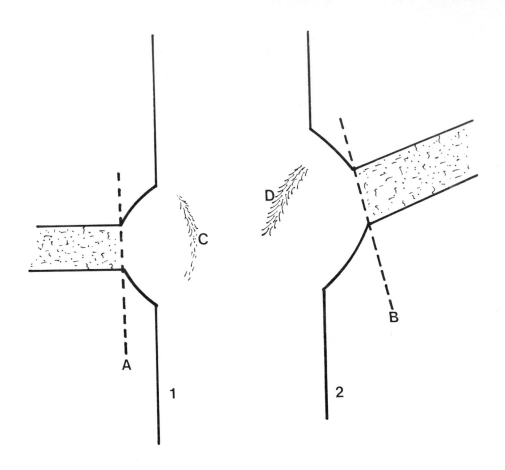

PROPER REMOVAL OF DEAD BRANCHES

To remove dead branches, make cuts as close as possible to the ring of sound wood about the branches; on conifers (1A) and hardwoods (2B). The branch bark ridges stop forming after the branches die (C and D). The ring of sound wood about the dead branches may be very large or very small and flat.

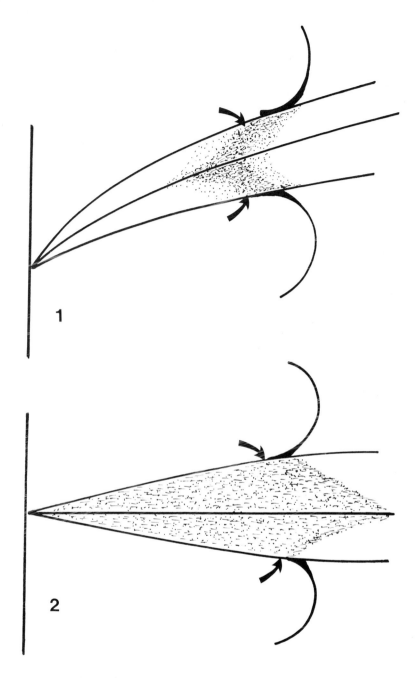

INSIDE VIEW OF DEAD BRANCHES

1. Branch protection zone in hardwoods (arrows).
2. Resin-soaked protection zone in conifers (arrows). The zone may extend into the branch stub.

Maine

DO NOT REMOVE THE BRANCH PROTECTION ZONE

When the branch protection zone is removed, pathogens spread rapidly into the tree. After injury and infection, trees form boundaries.

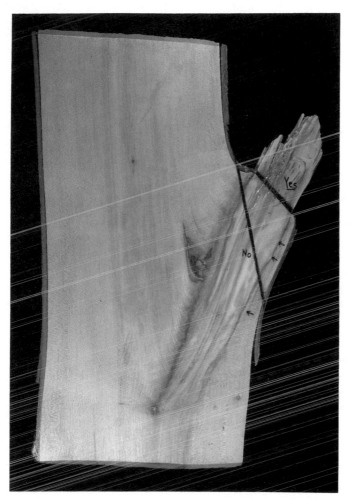

New Hampshire

DO NOT BREAK BOUNDARIES

A proper cut is along the "yes" line.

An improper cut along the "no" line will destroy the boundary that walls off the rotted wood.

If a hollow forms where there is rot now, and water fills the hollow, do not drill holes to drain the water. Water does not cause rot. You can siphon out the water and fill the cavity, but do not break the boundaries during the treatment.

New Hampshire

DEAD BRANCHES AND DISCOLORED WOOD

Discolored wood associated with the dead branch on the oak developed only downward. The discolored wood spread in the wood present at the time the branch died. Pathogens do not spread freely in sapwood or heartwood. Note the sound heartwood that formed after the branch died. The heartrot concept implies that pathogens spread freely in heartwood. This is not so.

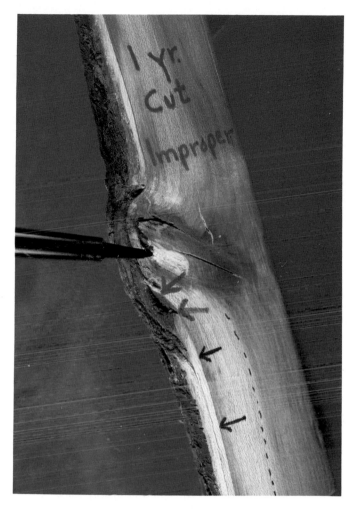

Maine

DO NOT REMOVE LIVING WOOD ABOUT DEAD BRANCHES

The ring of living wood about the small dead branch on this cherry was removed one year before the photo was taken. The dotted line shows the limits of the discolored wood before the branch was removed. The red arrow shows the size of the cut. The green arrow shows the dieback. The black arrows show the discolored wood that formed after the cut was made.

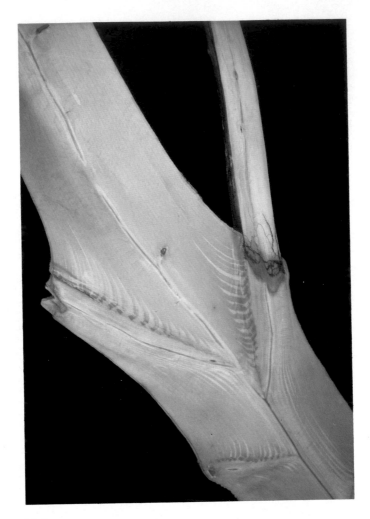

Maine

ROT PATTERNS A and B AFTER BRANCH DEATH

There are three patterns of rot development after branch death: A, B, and C.

A. Rot does not spread beyond the branch protection zone (left).

B. Rot begins to spread into the branch core (right).

ROT PATTERN C AFTER BRANCH DEATH
C. Rot spreads into the trunk wood present at the time of branch death.

ROT PATTERNS A, B, AND C AFTER BRANCH DEATH AND PATTERN D AFTER FLUSH CUTS

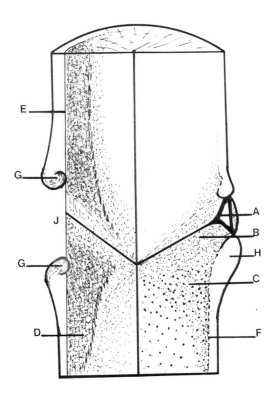

A. *Branch protection zone.* When proper cuts are made or when small branches die on trees, rot seldom spreads beyond the branch protection zone.

B. *Branch corewood.* When stubs remain on trees or when medium-sized dead branches remain on trees, rot may spread into the corewood. Corewood is the cone of branch tissues within the trunk.

C. *Trunk infection.* When large stubs or dead branches remain on trees, the rot may spread into the trunk tissues present at the time the branch died.

D. *Flush cuts and rot.* Flush cuts (J) remove the tissues that would produce the branch protection zone. The cuts injure the trunk above and below the branch. Rot develops rapidly into the trunk (D).

Barrier zones (E and F) separate infected wood from sound wood that continues to form after the cuts are made. Woundwood about proper cuts (H) does not roll inward. Woundwood about flush cuts (G) often rolls inward and starts internal vertical cracks. The cracks may later split outward when temperature extremes occur.

REMOVAL OF DEAD BRANCHES IS A HEALTH AND SAFETY TREATMENT.

Boundaries resist, not stop, spread of pathogens.

Removal of dying and dead branches takes away the food source for pathogens that could spread into the tree.

New Hampshire

DO NOT LEAVE LIVING STUBS

Living stubs have no defense system.
Many organisms attack dying tissues and spread into the tree.
The worst problem for man or trees is to be alive but have no defense system.
Do not do it to trees!

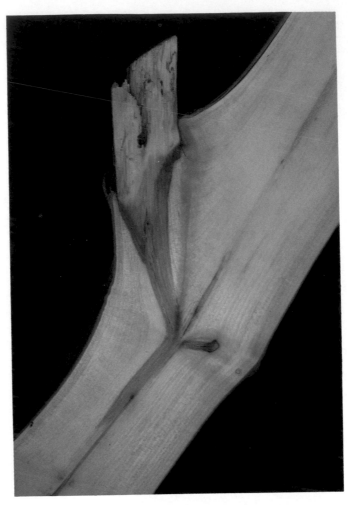

New Hampshire

DO NOT LEAVE DEAD STUBS

Dead stubs provide food and shelter for microorganisms and insects that could spread into the tree. If dead stubs are on trees, remove them by making cuts as close as possible to the ring of living wood at the base of the stub.

In the natural forest most twigs and branches die slowly when they are small. There is time for the branch protection zone to form. When large living branches are cut and stubs are left, the branch protection zone begins to form at the same time as organisms are spreading inward from the stub. Proper pruning leaves no stubs, and gives the branch protection zone time to form. The branch collar is not a stub.

Denmark

CALLUS CONFUSION

A large pocket of rot was behind the large ring of woundwood in the horse chestnut. *Callus is undifferentiated tissue with very little lignin. Woundwood is differentiated tissue with lignin.*

Confusion over woundwood (callus) as a sign of healing has been a major problem with pruning for centuries. People thought large "callus" meant strong healing.

This is why pruning cuts were made through the branch collar; a large "callus" formed. People knew about the branch protection zone for centuries. But, they still thought that "callus" as healing was more important. They also knew that rot developed rapidly when such a treatment was done. But, they felt that some magic wound dressing would stop the rot. That magic material has not yet come. And what has been called callus is really woundwood. Confusion indeed! (Niels Hvass)

California

WOUNDWOOD AND ROT FUNGUS

The fruit body of a rot fungus indicates advanced rot behind the large wound-wood rings on the coral tree.

People still believe that trees heal and that "callus" is a sign of healing. Healing means to restore tissues to their previous healthy state in the same spatial position. Trees do not do this. Every time a tree is wounded it is infected.

Trees cannot prevent infections. Trees wall off infections. Trees compartmentalize.

Sweden

WOUNDWOOD AND CAVITIES

Large cavities with large woundwood rings are often the result of large flush cuts. Too often while the cavity is being dug out, the same person makes more flush cuts.

Do not break boundaries while cleaning cavities.

Wound dressings protect the rot fungi. It is not possible to sterilize wood exposed by wounds and to keep it sterile. Also, there is no need to sterilize tools when cutting woody tissue. Tools should be sterilized when cutting nonwoody tissues on trees that have fire blight. Sterilize tools in household bleach, not alcohol.

West Germany

ALMOST-CLOSED WOUNDS

Large woundwood ribs give the appearance of closure. Liquids flowing from the wound indicate internal problems. An almost-closed wound creates perfect internal conditions for many organisms.

New Hampshire

WOUNDWOOD, SEALING, AND BOUNDARIES

When woundwood seals wounds and when internal protection boundaries are strong, rot, if it develops, will be walled off—compartmentalized.

People heal. Trees compartmentalize. People can rid themselves of infections. Every injury and infection a tree receives will be in the tree for the life of the tree.

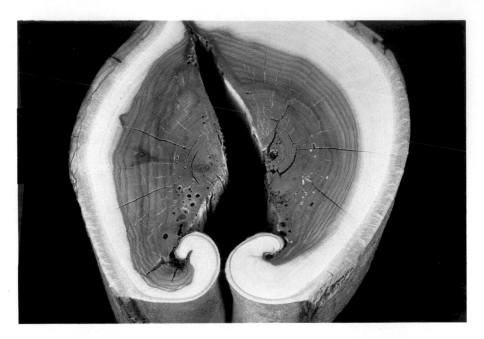

New Hampshire

WOUNDWOOD AND PROBLEMS

When woundwood forms rapidly and rolls inward — rams horn — the wound will never seal.

Internal cracks often form as the woundwood rolls inward. Flush cuts and many types of wound dressings stimulate rapid woundwood formation and all the problems that start when woundwood rolls inward.

WOUNDWOOD AND ROT

Rot forms in wood present at the time of injury. Woundwood forms after injury. Woundwood is the same size on all 3 wounds from the same maple tree. The amount of rot behind each wound is different. Development of rot and development of woundwood are two different processes.

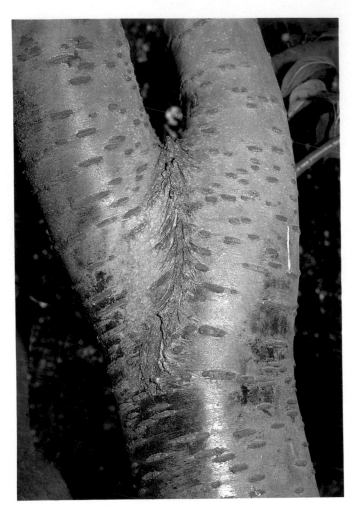

Washington

CODOMINANT STEMS

Codominant stems are stems growing at the same rate from the same position on another stem: forked stems. Codominant stems, unlike branches, do not have collars that form protection zones. A stem bark ridge forms between the stems. When the stem bark ridge turns upward as shown here, there is a strong union between the stems regardless of the angle of the stems.

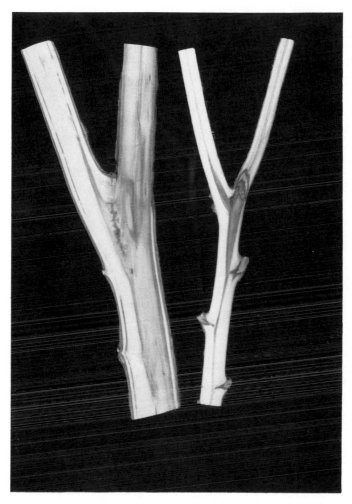

New Hampshire

CODOMINANT STEMS AND INFECTIONS

When a codominant stem is infected, defense boundaries resist spread of pathogens into the trunk.

At right, the fungus that causes Dutch elm disease was walled off in the trunk. At left, the right codominant stem was infected by the same fungus. It spread into the trunk tissues present at the time of death of the stem. The fungus did not spread to the left of the trunk.

Italy

CODOMINANT STEMS WITH WEAK UNIONS

When the stem bark ridge turns inward or when there is a crack between the stems, there is a weak union regardless of the angle of the stems. Do not buy trees that have weak unions between stems.

Angle of stem alone is not an indicator of a strong or weak union. However, when stems grow close together to form tight crotches, the chances for included bark and weak unions increases.

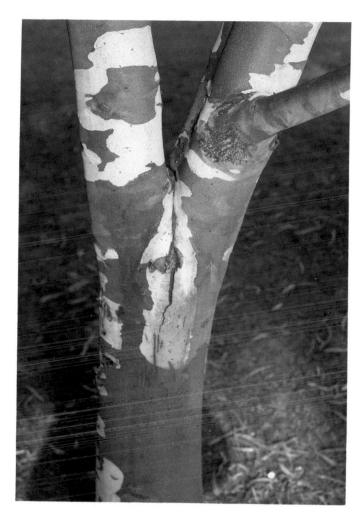

Australia

CODOMINANT STEMS AND CRACKS

Cracks between codominant stems are signs of weakness. On young trees, one of the stems could be removed. Or, one stem could be pruned more than the other. The stem with more pruning will grow slower and the other stem will form a collar about it. On older trees it may be possible to have the stems braced by professionals. Remove trees that cannot be braced.

Canada

CRACKS AND HAZARDS

Trees with large deep cracks should be removed by professionals. Cracks are major causes of hazard trees.

PROPER PRUNING OF CODOMINANT STEMS

1. To remove stem L, cut from C to D or from D to C with care.

   To remove stem M, cut from A to B or from B to A with care.

   Always stub cut the stem to be removed, and then make the final cut with care.

   Points D and B are opposite point E.

   Point E is the beginning of the stem bark ridge (J).

   Point C is to the left of the stem bark ridge and point A is to the right of the stem bark ridge.

   Never remove both stems.

2. When the bark plates on the stem bark ridge turn upward as shown in figure 1, the union of the stems is strong. When the bark between the stems turns inward as shown by K in figure 2, the union of the stems is weak. It is the union of the stems more than the angle that determines whether a stem is weak or strong. Strong unions usually have a U-shaped crotch.

   In figure 2, stem N is beginning to envelop stem O. The stems have bark between them at position K.

   The bark between the stems is called included bark.

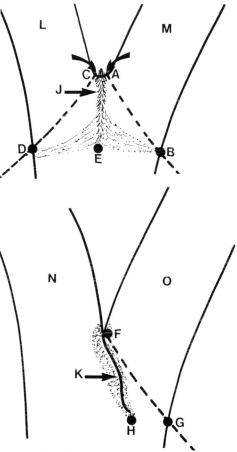

   There are three ways to remedy this situation: remove O, prune living wood from O and not from N, or put a cable between N and O.

   To remove O, stub cut the stem first and then cut from G to F with care. Point G is opposite point H, which is the beginning of the stem bark ridge, or the point where the bark begins to turn inward.

   To slow the growth of O, remove approximately a third of the living branches. Do not prune stem N. Stem N will begin to form a trunk collar about stem O. This can be done only on young trees.

   To strengthen stem O on older trees, a cable can be attached by professionals. The cable should be placed at a point approximately two-thirds of the distance from the crotch to the top of the tree.

   Proper placement of cables requires a great amount of skill. When a cable is used to strengthen stems, the cable must be checked regularly. When the risk of stem fracture becomes high, the stem should be removed by professionals.

New Hampshire

PROPER PRUNING OF A CODOMINANT STEM

The stem bark ridge is the key to proper pruning of codominant stems.
Do not leave stem stubs. They will be alive without a defense system.

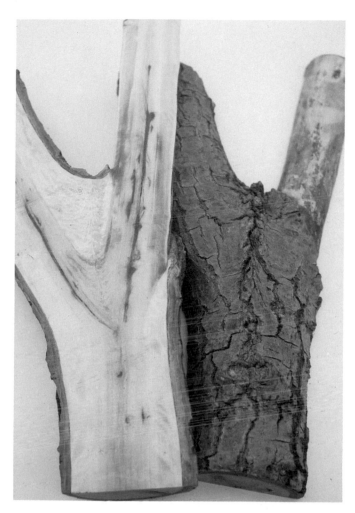

Italy

INSIDE VIEW OF A CODOMINANT STEM

Rot did not spread from the dead codominant stem, at right, deep into the trunk. The living ring of wood about the dead stem should not be injured when removing the stem.

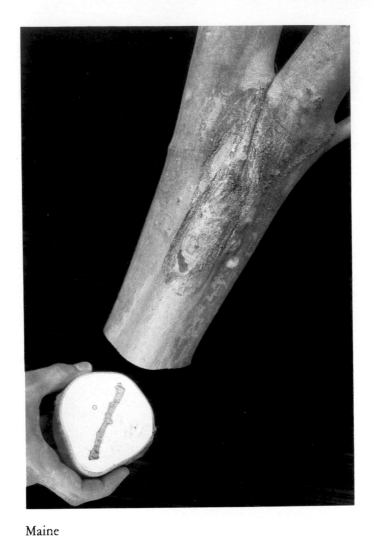

Maine

CODOMINANT STEMS AND INCLUDED BARK

Included bark is bark that is squeezed between stems. Included bark leads to weak unions. If a tree has a few branches with included bark, remove them as soon as possible.

California

INCLUDED BARK AND BRANCH FAILURE

When branches with included bark grow from a vertical to a horizontal direction they may split from the trunk. Trees with such defects should never be planted in cities.

Maryland   *Courtesy, Walter Money*

BRANCH CLUSTERS

Trees with clusters of branches low on the trunk look beautiful when young. As the branches grow into each other, included bark results.

Branch failure is common on such trees.

Florida

INCLUDED BARK AND HAZARDS

Be on guard for large trunks or branches with included bark that are growing away from the main trunk. They are extreme hazards. (Robert Kyle)

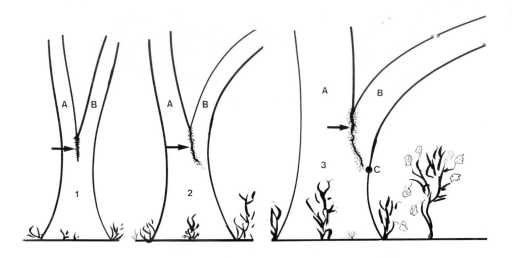

INCLUDED BARK AND DANGER

1.   When A and B grow in a vertical direction and the stem bark ridge (arrow) is straight down from a U-shaped crotch, the hazard risk for fracture between the stems is low.

2.   When stem B begins to grow away from stem A and the stem bark ridge begins to curve toward the base of stem B (arrow), the hazard risk for fracture between the stems is moderate.

3.   When stem B grows away from stem A, and a crack forms between the stems (arrow), the hazard risk for fracture between the stems is high.

Be on guard when stem B begins to grow over roads, walkways, recreation areas or other places where people and vehicles could be injured or damaged if the stem failed.

Stem B may be strengthened by a cable when it begins to grow away from stem A as shown in figure 2.

When a crack forms between stem A and stem B, as shown in figure 3, stem B should be removed by professionals. Always stub cut stem B first. Follow directions for removal of stems with included bark. On large trees, stem B may be removed by making a cut from C inward to the included bark. The final cut must be made with the tip of the chainsaw, which can be very dangerous. Great care must be taken if that type of cut is made.

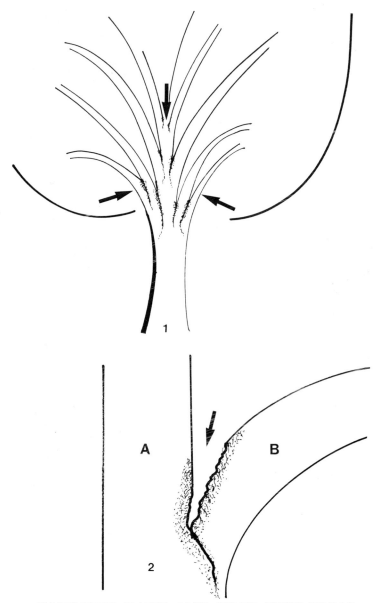

INCLUDED BARK AND POOR TREE FORM

1. Do not buy trees that have many branches with included bark, especially if the branches are in a cluster near the lower portion of the trunk (arrows).

2. When cracks begin to form between A and B (arrow), remove B as soon as possible.

   If only a few branches on a tree have included bark, remove them as soon as possible.

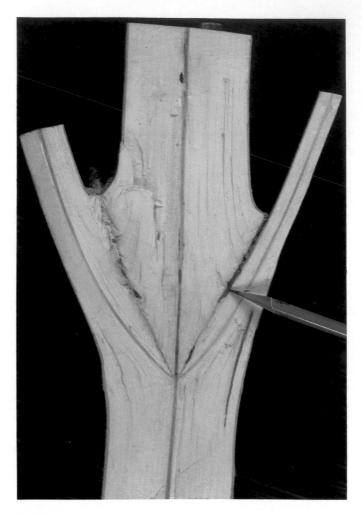

Maine

INSIDE VIEW OF INCLUDED BARK

Included bark in a maple is shown by the pencil. The branches were growing at the same angle. Branches with included bark should be removed while the tree is young.

Maine

INCLUDED BARK BETWEEN A PINE BRANCH AND TRUNK

Dead spots may develop on all species of trees as the cambium of both the trunk and branch are squeezed and killed.

North Carolina

PROPER PRUNING OF A BRANCH WITH INCLUDED BARK
The holly branch with included bark was pruned properly. Woundwood did not form at the top of the wound.

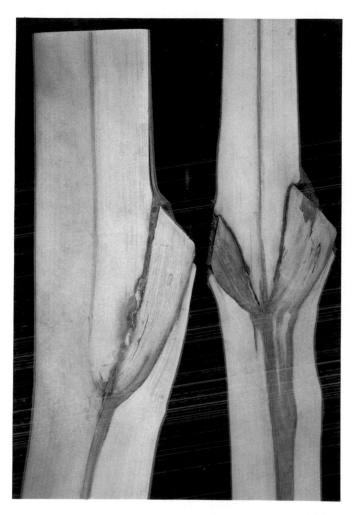

Maine

INSIDE VIEW OF PROPER PRUNING OF BRANCHES WITH INCLUDED BARK

Remove branches with included bark as soon as possible on young trees.
Do not injure the trunk. Some rot may develop in the branch cores as shown here. If a hollow develops as the core is rotted, do not drill holes to drain the water.

California

GOOD TREE FORM

This tree has good form for a specimen tree away from cars and people. Some pruning of small branches is needed.

Buy trees that have stem bark ridges and branch bark ridges that turn upward. Do not plant trees with low branches where people and vehicles move by.

Trees with strong central leaders are best for planting near walkways and streets. Trees with many strong codominant stems starting low on the trunk are best for planting near power lines or where short trees are wanted.

California

POOR TREE FORM

Be on guard when branches grow from a vertical to a horizontal direction, especially when they have included bark as shown here. Some corrective pruning can be done on young trees. Start with good form and prune to keep it that way. It will save you time, money, and maybe the pain of going to court.

Switzerland

CORRECTION OF POOR FORM

This tree looks beautiful now, but it will grow into a problem unless some corrective pruning is done soon. Tips of lateral branches should be pruned to establish a strong central leader. As the new leader with higher lateral branches forms, the lower branches now on the tree should be removed.

Washington

START WITH GOOD FORM

For cities, buy trees that have a strong central leader. Tip prune lateral branches and later remove the lateral branches as the leader grows. When the right tree is put in the right place and given enough room to grow, and not planted too deep, it will seldom crack sidewalks or streets.

When trees begin to form many codominant stems, height growth will decrease. If short trees are wanted, start pruning early to establish many codominant stems with strong unions. It can be done.

Denmark

KNOW WHEN TO CULL

There are times when the best pruning treatments will still not solve the problem. To remove the right stem on this tree would not only leave a large wound but the tree would be unsightly. Trees have dignity. This tree should be replaced. It is a tree that will grow into a hazard tree because of the weak crotch.

California

YOUR MONEY WASTED

Your money is wasted when cities buy trees like this. And when a branch falls and injures a person, the blame is put on nature or "Act of God". It is time to put the blame where it belongs.

Tell the nurseries in very clear terms what kinds of trees you will accept.

Do not accept trees that have poor form.

New Hampshire

PROPER TRAINING CUTS ON YOUNG TREES

Proper training cuts on young and small trees often involve removal of vertical leader stems and ends of lateral branches. Proper training cuts are made at nodes. A node is the place where branches are attached to trunks or where branches are attached to other branches. An internode is the trunk or branch section between nodes. Never make internodal cuts.

Training cuts are necessary for espalier, topiary, pleaching, fruit trees and other designs. Here is a proper training cut on a young tree.

Pleaching is a pruning treatment where branches are woven together to form a bower or arbor. The treatment is a variation on the theme of pollarding.

PROPER TRAINING CUT
TO REMOVE A LEADER
ON A YOUNG TREE

To remove the leader stem on a young, small tree, cut from A to B.

Always stub cut the stem H first.

Point A is to the inside of the branch bark ridge (J) within the branch crotch.

Point B is opposite point F.

Point F is the beginning of the branch bark ridge.

Point K is the branch collar, and G is the branch that will become the new leader.

Improper cuts are A to E, A to D, C to E, C to B, and C to D.

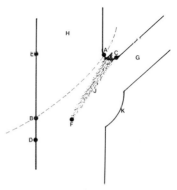

TRAINING YOUNG, SMALL TREES

Most young, small trees can be trained to grow in many different shapes. Start with a tree that has the basic framework and growth pattern to give you what you want.

All cuts should be made properly at nodes.

To have a tree with a long trunk, start early in the life of the tree to remove branches at positions 1, 2, and 3. Do not remove more than a third of the living branches.

For a more compact tree, remove C's.

For a more upright tree, remove A's.

For a more open tree, remove B's.

To regulate height, remove D at position 6.

If a tree with a strong central leader is wanted, remove other upright stems at position 6 that may be competing with D.

If a large portion of the top must be removed, make the cut at a node where there is a strong side branch.

These training cuts are only for young, small trees.

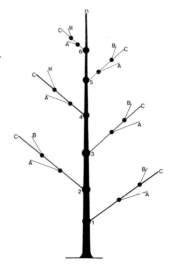

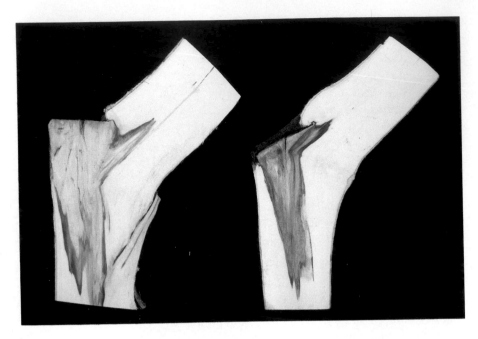

Maine

PROPER AND IMPROPER TRAINING CUTS
Rot spread rapidly after the improper flat-top cut (left).
A small core of discolored wood formed after a proper cut (right).
The samples are maple with 3-year-old cuts.

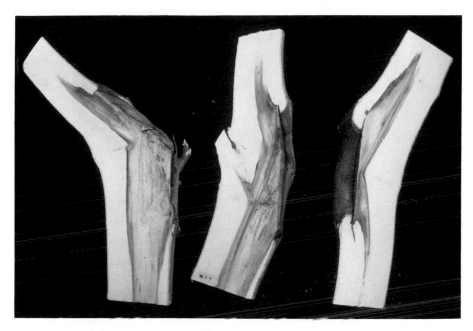

TRAINING CUT TOO CLOSE

When training cuts are made too close, rot spreads rapidly upward and downward. The samples are maple with 3-year-old cuts.

Canada

TOPPING LARGE TREES: CRIME AGAINST NATURE

Topping is the removal of vertical leader stems on large trees.

Topping cuts are usually made between nodes or at internodes.

Tipping is an internodal cut on large lateral branches.

Topping and tipping of large trees causes serious injury no matter how the cuts are made. People often want trees to grow big, fast. And, when they do, people want them small again. The wrong tree in the wrong place is a major reason for tipping and topping. The practice leads to hazardous trees.

France

TOPPING, ROT, AND CRACKS

Topping often leads to top rot and long cracks. Lightning often gets blamed.
People often want to top trees because they feel that the tree will become a hazard.
Topping greatly increases the hazard risk of the tree.

Italy

TOPPING AND ROOT PROBLEMS

Wounds made by topping cuts weaken tissues from the trunk to the roots. Pathogens that cause rots and root diseases infect the weakened wood.

When tree tops are removed, roots begin to starve. Many opportunistic pathogens will infect starving roots. The primary pathogen is the person who removed the tree top!

Australia

TOPPING AND SPROUTS

Topping stimulates excessive sprouting. The sprouts are unsightly and hazardous. Topping trees under power lines causes more sprouts to grow back into the lines faster.

Excessive sprouting is a sign of low energy reserves.

Australia

TOPPING, SPROUTS, CAVITIES: HAZARDS

Topping, sprouts, and cavities lead to dangerous hazard conditions. Sprouts have a very weak union on trunks. Be on guard for sprouts that are growing rapidly in a horizontal direction.

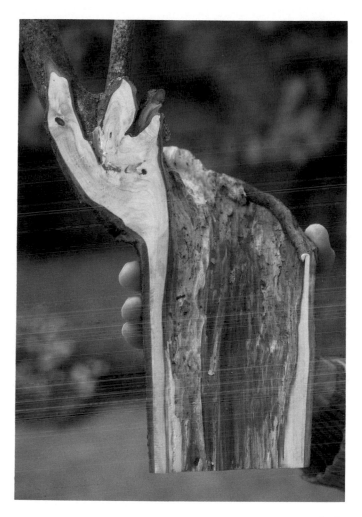

Italy

TOPPING AND BRANCH FAILURE

Be on guard for sprouts growing rapidly on rotted trunks. This is a common cause of branch failure in fruit trees.

Plant young trees as old trees begin to age and die. Removal of the old trees will not leave large open spots in the landscape.

West Germany

TRAINING CUTS AND POLLARDING

Proper pollarding starts with proper training cuts. Know the tree design you want *before* you start. Start with a tree species that lends itself to that design. Proper pollarding requires *constant* attention. One type of pollard design has a single stem, as shown here.

The tree shown is a globose variety of Norway maple. It is a good garden tree.

Washington

SINGLE STEM POLLARD

Care must be taken not to cut into the pollard head or rot will develop into the trunk. The same precautions must be taken for grapevines, wisterias, and other plants that are pollarded.

Italy

BRANCHING POLLARD

Another type of pollard design starts with a branching framework. Design the framework by making proper training cuts at the unions of branches. The framework must be started when the tree is young and small.

Courtesy, Niels Hvass   Denmark

POLLARD MAINTENANCE

The pollard head must be pruned properly every year. It is still a very economical treatment because the trees stay healthy, beautiful, and safe for many years. More proper pollarding should be done with trees near power lines.

When sprouts from pollard heads grow for three or more years and then are removed, the tree roots begin to starve. Some trees tolerate such treatment, but rot and root diseases often develop. The treatment is the same as topping.

Switzerland

IMPROPER POLLARDING

This is not pollarding. It is tree mutilation. Too often tree mutilation is called pollarding. Pollarding is a fine pruning practice that takes a great amount of skill. Over the life of the tree, the treatment is very economical.

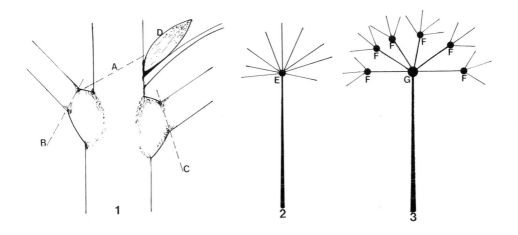

STARTING A POLLARD

Proper pollarding must start when the tree is small and young — 2 to 4 meters tall and 4 to 8 cm. in diameter at one meter above the ground.

Some trees lend themselves to pollarding — Linden, London Plane, Catalpa, Horse Chestnut. Some trees tolerate the treatment.

To start a single trunk pollard, remove the young, small branches properly during the dormant season, figure 1, B and C. Some upright stems or leader stems must be removed. Proper cuts below buds (D) on some stems must be made (A). The height of the single trunk pollard head must be determined at the first pruning (figure 2, E).

Sprouts will grow from the pruning cuts. At the end of the growing season, the sprouts should be removed, (figure 2, E).

A multiple head pollard may be started in two basic ways. The procedures used to establish the single-trunk pollard can be repeated on the same tree (figure 3). The sprouts must be cut back to F at the end of every growing season.

Another way to start a multiple head pollard is to establish the heads as given for a single trunk pollard, but start many of them on a slightly older and larger tree. And, again, once the positions of the heads are determined, the sprouts must be cut back to the heads at the end of every growing season.

In some cases, one or two sprouts may be left on the pollard heads to give the tree a lace-like appearance as it begins to grow.

When removing sprouts, do not injure the pollard heads. Do not leave stubs. Make cuts as close as possible to the swollen collars that surround each sprout.

109

South Korea

SHAPING

Trees can be trained by pruning to have many shapes. Do not design shapes that shade lower portions of the plant. Pruning to maintain a topiary must be done several times a year. Constant pruning will prevent dead spots. Remove dead wood by making cuts deep into the plant where dead wood joins living wood.

ESPALIER

Espalier starts by planting the tree close to a wall or some type of vertical support. Remove the top when the desired height is reached. Select lateral branches early that will be the basic framework. Constant pruning is necessary to maintain the shape and growth rate. When pruning starts early in the life of a plant and continues, the root system will adapt to the mass of the tree.

New Hampshire

TRAINING YOUNG TREES

Proper removal of tips of branches at nodes on young trees is essential for establishing a framework. Know where the buds are. Some trees have buds along the stem as shown here. Other trees have buds at the tips of the stems. Make slanted cuts just above a bud. Do not leave stubs of wood beyond a bud. On branches, always cut at nodes where one branch has a union with another branch. Do not leave branch stubs. Do not make flush cuts.

Italy

SHEARING

Shearing is not a good practice. Some trees such as yews tolerate it. Removal of apical buds before they begin to grow will result in more growth of lateral buds. Shearing too deep into the plant will result in dead twigs. The dead twigs should be removed at the point of union with a living stem. To avoid dead spots, it is best to shear after growth begins. On some pines the candles of new growth can be sheared as they begin to grow.

Italy

PRUNING WOODY VINES

Most grapes grown for wine are grown on a few selected vines from a pollard head. Most table grapes are grown on long vines on some support or trellis. The basic rules are the same. Establish the framework first. Then prune back to pollard heads as shown here with the wisteria, or to the basic framework.

Oregon

FRUIT TREE PRUNING

Fruit trees are pruned many different ways. Citrus in large orchards are often sheared to facilitate harvesting. The cuts should not go deep into the tree. Do not shear fruit trees growing in your yard. Shearing is not a good practice for fruit trees. Many fruit trees are trained as espalier. The open center design with large spreading lateral branches is common. Remove vertical shoots or buds to establish a framework. Branches may be tied as shown here.

Fruit trees are often pruned harshly to stimulate fruit production. The trees then die.

Denmark

PLANT PROPERLY

Know what you want. Know your site. Select a tree that will be right for you and your site. Get advice from professionals. Prepare a planting site, not just a small hole. Plant at the depth the tree grew in the nursery. Do not plant too deep! Do not amend the soil unless you have very poor soil or building rubble. It is better to plant on a site where you must add water than on a site where you must drain water. Keep grass away. If you build a water dam, remove it after the tree becomes established.

Florida

PROPER BRACING

If your tree requires bracing, use broad strapping that will not injure the bark. Do not use wire in a hose. The tree should move slightly. Remove braces as soon as the tree is well rooted.

Do not put wires in the crotches of branches as shown here.

Maryland

PRUNING AFTER PLANTING

At planting time remove branches and roots that are injured or diseased. Do not try to prune to balance crown area with root area! Wait until the tree begins to grow. Then prune dying branches. Fertilize the tree lightly after the tree forms mature needles or leaves.

When you plant a tree, you become responsible for it. Start a maintenance program after you plant the tree, and keep it up. It will save you money and it will help the tree to be healthy, beautiful, and safe for many years.

Australia

PRUNING BIG, OLD TREES

Pruning big, old trees is a job for professionals. Remove dead and dying branches first. Then remove branches that have weak unions or branches that are rubbing another branch. Do not tip prune living branches and leave dead, dying and defective branches.

There are no sound rules to tell you how much living tissue to remove. If you have the same amount of leaves or needles on a short branch as on a long branch you can remove more living tissue from the short branch. Leaves must provide food for all the living cells in the branch wood, trunk, and roots. Watch trees after you prune. If many sprouts form, too much living tissue was removed.

As trees grow older, the amount of healthy living tissue removed by pruning should decrease.

119

West Germany

OVER PRUNING INJURES LARGE, OLD TREES

This tree has been injured seriously. It has been over pruned.

Many terms, such as crown reduction, drop crotch pruning, lateral branch pruning, are really topping and tipping and over pruning as shown here. The crown on most large, old trees can be thinned by removing dead, dying, and defective branches. With most old trees this is usually all that is needed. The exception is a living branch that is a hazard. All cuts should be at crotches. Removing large vertical stems at internodes is topping no matter what the size of the branch is below the cut. Removing tips of large branches at internodes is tipping no matter how it is done.

Over pruning leaves a tree injured biologically and mechanically. Over pruning leads to root problems. Do not over prune mature trees!

North Carolina

OVER PRUNING AND SPROUTS

Excessive sprouting is a sign of over pruning. Sprouts usually grow from dormant buds. Some sprouts grow rapidly and persist. They are elites. Other sprouts grow for a few years and die. They are the suppressed sprouts. If sprouts are to be removed, wait until the elites are obvious. Cut the suppressed sprouts. Do not injure the tissues that hold the sprouts. The branch shown has received many flush cuts. The sun was blamed for the dead spots.

Florida

TIPPING, TOPPING, AND PROBLEMS

Repeated tipping and topping have not only injured this tree, but have made the tree into a hazard. There is no way to make a big tree small again! The only answer is to plant new trees and start a training program early. When the new trees are established, then the big tree should not be there.

If you want fast growing trees, plant them on a short rotation plan. Every 10 or 15 years, the trees could be replaced.

Australia

TIPPING, TOPPING, AND POWER LINE PROBLEMS

Tipping can lead to serious hazards, especially when the sprouts grow over streets or walkways. Tipping and topping near power lines leads to excessive sprouting. The sprouts grow rapidly into the lines. Do not plant trees under power lines. Or plant small maturing species. Or start pruning when the trees are small. (Nicholas Rivett)

Washington

SPROUTS AND HAZARDS

Be on guard for sprouts growing on rotted trunks. The only answer is to remove the tree and plant new trees. Tipping and topping destroy the tree's defense systems. The practice may lead to litigation when falling branches or trunks injure people. Programs of regular pruning save money, and they may even save lives.

FLUSH CUTS AND HAZARDS

This photo shows one of the most dangerous conditions on trees. The flush cut starts internal cracks. The cracks often lead to branch failure.

It is better to remove a large lateral branch at the trunk than to take many branches off the lateral branch. This is important for pruning near power lines.

Sprouts growing from the branch are often called "dog tails".

Switzerland

PROPER REGULATION OF SIZE AND SHAPE

Proper training has kept this tree attractive, and the same size and shape for many years. The method is a variation on pollarding. The framework was established early and the sprouts are pruned back to the framework every year.

The tree, the tree owner, and the person doing the pruning all benefit from such a regular maintenance program.

Florida

IMPROPER PRUNING TO REGULATE SIZE AND SHAPE

The tips of the branches were pruned too late in the life of this tree. Small pollard heads formed at the tips rather than small bud clusters along the branch.

The answer is easy: establish the framework early in the life of the tree. The action is difficult: people wait too long.

Sweden

WOUND DRESSING MYTHS

There are no data to show that wound dressings stop rot. They do stall defense systems and protect the rot fungi. If branches are pruned properly, the tree will form protective zones on the inside.

If some colored material is wanted for cosmetics, make certain that the material is not toxic, and apply a very thin coat.

If the wound is left without a dressing, the surface will hardly be noticeable in one year and will look the same as the tree bark. (Ollie Andersen and Klaus Vollbrecht)

West Germany

WOUND DRESSINGS AND ROT

The pruning cut shown here was proper at the top but too close at the bottom. After one year there was no infection at the top but infection at the bottom. The fungi did not infect the branch core. It was the nature of the cut, and not the wound dressing, that prevented infection at the top.

This type of cut, proper at top and very close below, is perfect for wildlife cavities. Add wound dressing to develop the cavity faster!

West Germany

WOUND DRESSINGS PROTECT MICROORGANISMS

When wound dressings are applied over wounds that are already infected, the dressing protects the microorganisms.

Be on guard for people who climb your tree with climbing spikes. The wounds injure the tree and deface the trunk. Or, if they insist on wound dressing, insist that every spike wound be scribed and painted. We must be consistent!!!

California

WOUND DRESSINGS, FLUSH CUTS, AND HAZARDS

Fruit bodies of rot fungi on flush cuts coated with wound dressing signal extreme hazard. The tree shown here was along a city street. The wound dressing gives a false sign of security. Wound dressings are a waste of time and money.

Question: If flush cuts and wound dressings are so good, why are there so many cavities after the practice is done?

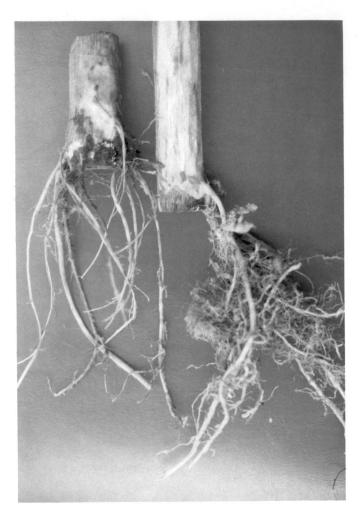

Maine

ROOT PRUNING

When woody roots are cut, new roots generate. Roots compartmentalize as well as trunks and branches.

When roots are crushed during construction work, make new smooth-surface cuts as soon as possible. When root pruning, remember that most new roots will grow outward from the cut root. Do not remove the new roots when digging the tree for transplanting.

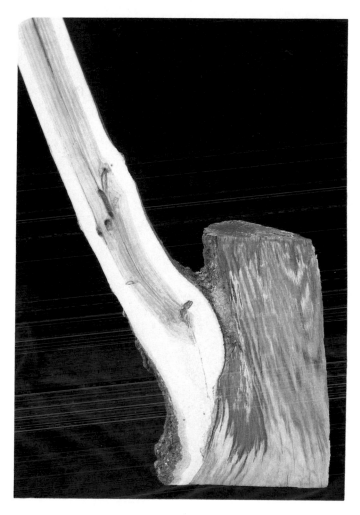

Maine

STUMP SPROUTS

After a tree is cut, sprouts may grow from dormant buds, or from adventitious buds. Single sprouts low on the stump grow to be the best trees. Rot does not spread from the old stump to the sprout. Note how the bark of the sprout separates the sprout from the stump.

When cutting trees to produce sprouts for coppice growth or for biomass, make the first cut at the ground line. When removing sprouts later, cut as close as possible to the wood that produced the sprout, but do not cut into the wood. A type of pollard head forms at ground line. Pollard heads should not be injured.

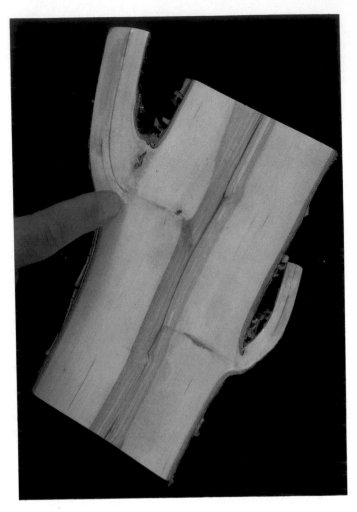

New Hampshire

EPICORMIC BUDS AND SPROUTS

Epicormic means "upon a trunk". There are 2 types of epicormic buds: dormant buds that are formed in the axils of leaves and remain in the cambial zone as the tree grows, and adventitious buds that form anew within the cambial zone and callus after wounding.

Epicormic sprouts have weak unions. The finger points to an epicormic sprout. The union with the trunk is similar to a branch with included bark.

New Hampshire

WILDLIFE AND PRUNING

All the deadwood was removed from this hickory tree except the snag on top. The snag is a popular perch site for birds. Within the limits of safety, keep wildlife in mind when you prune.

Remember, large, old, healthy trees with a few cavities, and a few dead branches make the best wildlife trees.

New Hampshire

BONSAI

Bonsai — tree in a pot — is one of the most highly developed methods of regulating tree growth and shape. Bonsai proves that tree size and shape can be regulated by pruning, for hundreds of years. In the Orient, the bonsai method is used to keep trees one to four meters tall for over a hundred years.

For some bonsai designs, flush cuts are made to bring about the effect of injured and weathered old trees.

Bonsai must start when trees are young and small.

Australia

TREE DIGNITY

Trees, like all living things, grow old and die. Do not insult old trees with wound dressings and treatments that result in more metal and concrete than wood.

Let trees die with dignity.

Then plant new trees. And, maintain what you plant.

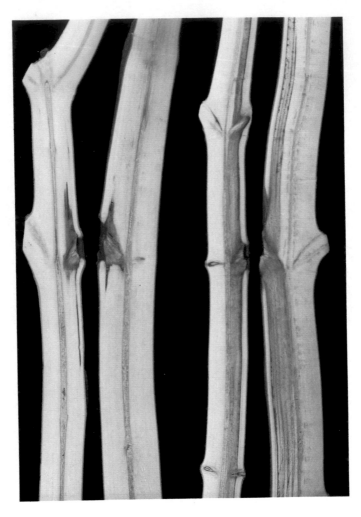

Maine

THE FUTURE

Some individual trees of a species compartmentalize more rapidly than others of the same species.

All 4 red maples shown here had 1-year-old flush cuts.

The 2 trees at right were weak. The 2 trees at left were strong. It is time to start selecting and planting strong trees in our forests and cities.

For at least two centuries some people understood the importance of the protection zone and the branch collar. These people regulated growth rate and shape by proper pruning. New information on how branches are attached to trunks was the missing link that put all the pieces of the pruning story together.

Holland

PEOPLE AND TREES

The subject of tree pruning is almost endless. Learn how trees grow and defend themselves.

Learn about trees by reading.

Learn by talking to people who understand and love trees.

Learn by touching trees. (Peter van der Bom)

TREES AND THEIR ASSOCIATES   Australia

Trees and their associates have lived for millions of years in forests. When we bring them into our world, we become responsible, forever, for their proper care. Pruning, properly done, is a major way to help trees stay healthy, attractive, and hazard free.

140

APPENDIX

HOW TREES GROW AND DEFEND THEMSELVES

The basic unit of life is the cell. The cell contains the substances of life. The cell contents are held in place by a boundary. In animals the boundary is thin. Skin holds the cells in place. A skeleton holds the skin in place. The system allows animals to move.

Tree cells have thick boundaries or walls. The walls consist mostly of cellulose and lignin. The strong cell walls make it possible for the tree to have superior mechanical support. Trees grow bigger and taller than any other organism ever to inhabit earth. Trees cannot move.

Trees stand in place and often receive many wounds. Trees cannot restore or heal wounded wood.

Animals heal. Heal means to restore to a previous healthy state in the same spatial position. After injury, animals restore, repair, replace, or regenerate injured cells. People who live a long life will restore parts of their cells and the cells themselves over 270 billion times.

Trees cannot restore cells one time. Trees are generating systems. Animals are regenerating systems. Animals survive as long as they can restore parts faster than they are breaking down.

Trees survive as long as they can form new parts in new positions faster than old parts are breaking down.

Trees survive after injury and infection by compartmentalizing the injured and infected tissues.

Compartmentalization is a tree defense process in which boundaries form that resist spread of pathogens. Boundaries also defend the liquid transport, energy storage, and mechanical support systems.

After injury and infection, stored energy substances in living cells are converted to substances that resist spread of pathogens. When wounds break through the bark, sapwood that has living cells is injured. When wounds break into heartwood that has no living cells, boundaries still form. How boundaries form in heartwood is not well understood.

The boundary that forms in wood present at the time of injury is called the reaction zone. After wounding, the still-living cambium about the wound forms a boundary called the barrier zone.

The reaction zone resists spread of pathogens within the tissues present at the time of injury and infection. The barrier zone separates the wood present at the time of injury from the new wood that forms in a new spatial position.

Healing is a one-part system. Healing is restoration in the same spatial position.

Compartmentalization is a two-part system. Compartmentalization is resistance of spread of pathogens, and the generation of new cells in new positions. Compartmentalization must have higher survival value than healing because most trees live much longer than any animal.

If trees have such a superior survival system, why do they not live even longer?

A generating system with boundaries has some advantages and disadvantages for long survival.

No living system can grow beyond the limits of energy available to operate the system.

Now we must look briefly at the laws of thermodynamics. The first law states that energy cannot be created or destroyed, only passed on in other forms. The second law states that any system that does not receive enough energy to maintain order will go to disorder. The third law deals with absolute states of energy.

The three laws can be paraphrased:
You can never win, only break even; you can only break even at absolute zero; and you can never reach absolute zero!

The missing ingredient is time. Life is a time game.

An organism stays alive so long as it has enough energy to grow and defend itself.

All living things have mass. Trees have two types of mass—static and dynamic.

All tissues of the tree that have some living cells make up the dynamic mass. Tissues that do not have living cells make up the static mass.

Trees regulate, in ways we do not understand, the ratio of dynamic to static mass. Trees shed nonwoody parts and parts that die. Some trees have wood that is altered during aging to a high state of protection—heartwood. Trees compartmentalize wood infected by pathogens—discolored wood, decayed wood, wetwood. In the natural forest the tree has two basic ways to survive under the rules of mass and energy. The tree may start life at a slow rate and continue to grow at a slow rate.

The other alternative is to grow rapidly until a dominant position in the canopy is reached. Then the tree forms many codominant stems. The top of the tree becomes rounded.

Trees in the natural forest die when they begin to grow rapidly, but do not grow rapidly enough to have a dominant position in the canopy. Here the dynamic mass begins to exceed the available energy. Before the tree dies of energy depletion, opportunistic pathogens enter and pass on the still available energy.

The same procedure operates for branches. Shade is an important factor for branch and tree death, but shade is only one of the factors. If this were not so, we would not find small, slow-growing trees growing in more shade than dying branches on larger trees of the same species.

A tall dominant or small dwarfed tree of the same species cannot grow beyond the one-to-one ratio of dynamic mass to available energy.

As a tree grows older, it is not only the increase in dynamic mass that becomes a problem. As the tree grows older, energy is required for reproduction. And, as branches and roots die and as more wounds are inflicted, the tree must use more energy for defense.

In a sense, each branch is a tree. The developing trunk provides space for each tree-branch to grow. But, the energy demands on the tree-branch increase as the trunk gets larger and as the woody roots get larger. The sapwood of the trunk and roots must get their energy from the leaves on the tree-branch. When the tree-branch begins to shed parts and become smaller, this is the beginning of the end for the tree-branch.

The young small tree does not have these problems. The young tree is all dynamic mass.

The information given here helps to explain why bonsai, espalier, and pollarding are pruning methods that keep trees at a set size for many years. The techniques keep the tree near the one-to-one ratio of mass to energy.

Knowing this helps to explain why a young tree tolerates many training cuts. Young trees can have many branches removed and the tree will still live in a healthy state. The same treatment to an old tree causes serious injury. This also explains why trees that grow out of their pollard state cannot be brought back without serious injury, usually to the roots.

Here are a few major summary points from this discussion:

People move. Anything that moves will wear out. People restore. So long as rate of restoration exceeds the rate of wearing down, and there is enough energy to maintain the ratio in favor of restoration, life will continue.

Trees do not move. Trees are generating systems. They get bigger. Anything that continues to increase in mass runs the risk of increasing mass beyond the energy available to operate the system. So long as the rate of generation of new parts in new positions exceeds the rate of breakdown of old parts in old positions; and there is enough energy to maintain the ratio in favor of generation, life will continue.

This means that you can regulate tree growth by proper pruning.

Pruning must start early in the life of the tree and it must be done at regular intervals depending on the desired design.

When you prune a tree you change the ratio of mass to energy. In young trees, the ratio is far in favor of energy. A great amount of living tissue could be removed in training and little injury will result. When you prune an older tree that has a one-to-one ratio of mass to energy, even small amounts of living tissues removed, harm the tree.

You cannot prune a big tree to make it a small healthy tree no matter how you try.

You can keep a small tree a healthy small tree, for a long time, by proper pruning.

But, no matter what you do, all living things will eventually die. However, proper treatment of all living systems will extend the time of high quality life!

143

WHAT KEEPS YOU ALIVE WILL EVENTUALLY KILL YOU.

The laws of thermodynamics can be paraphrased in another way. You can not live forever, only for a while. You can live while you maintain perfect order. You cannot always maintain perfect order.

Life is a time game against these laws.

Life is the momentary perfect order of movement within cells.

The unique feature of a tree is its strong mechanical support system. The strong cell wall gives every part of the tree strong individual support. And, because of this, trees grow bigger than any other organism. That is the good news.

Trees are generating systems. To stay alive they must keep forming new cells in new positions. Such a design would quickly bring a tree to death as mass would exceed energy available to maintain the mass.

Trees stay alive by regulating their mass. They shed parts and they alter older parts that become static mass.

But even with all of the checks and balances against mass exceeding energy, the inevitable still happens. Even at a ratio of one-to-one of mass to energy, the total tree—dynamic and static mass—keeps getting bigger.

A new threat enters: mechanical disruption. The tree begins to break apart. That is the bad news.

The tree design came about in the forest where trees grew close to other trees. There was one other check against mechanical disruption, trees protected each other by being close.

We have taken the tree out of the forest and planted it as an individual. This is a new condition for the tree. The city tree grows with large lower branches. The architecture of the tree is changed.

Tree health to many people means a fast-growing tree.

Now enters the tree problem again: mechanical disruption. The tree grows itself into problems. Wind, ice, and snow cause large branches to break.

Trees that begin to grow beyond their genetically programmed architecture are diseased.

A disease is any abnormal physiological or anatomical process that causes injury or death to an organism.

When a tree grows so big and so fast that it begins to exceed its mass to energy ratio, that tree is diseased! If the condition continues, that tree will die.

When a tree grows so big and so fast that parts begin to break because they exceed the architectural limits for tree structure, the part that breaks away dies. The wound left by the fracture injures the other parts of the tree.

So; are big and fast really better? Is this what we really want for our urban trees?

Proper pruning is a major way to help trees that can be threatened by the disease of overgrowth.

This is a major reason why we must prune trees that we bring into our world.

Pruning is so much more than removing branches. Pruning is understanding the tree to know what to remove, how much to remove, when to remove, how to remove, how often to remove, and how to treat the tree in other ways to maintain health and safety.

A human surgeon does more than just make the cut. The surgeon must understand the body.

We must understand the tree. Then proper pruning will become an art and a science. And it will be a matter of common sense!

HISTORY OF TREE PRUNING PROBLEMS

Pruning of trees is one of the oldest plant treatments. Man pruned trees to regulate size and shape and to improve the quantity and quality of flowers, fruit, and timber and to provide shade and windbreaks. All treatments were for the benefit of man.

Hundreds of books and scientific papers have been written on pruning. Why then do we see so much improper pruning? Here are some reasons.

Tree pruning developed as four independent practices, for gardens, orchards, forests, and bonsai.

Trees in gardens were pruned to regulate size and shape, and to increase flower quantity and beauty. Garden pruning gave us topiary, espalier, pleaching, and pollarding. All of these pruning practices took a great deal of time and skill, and they had to be repeated frequently.

Orchard pruning was done to increase the quantity and quality of fruit and to facilitate harvesting.

Forest tree pruning was done to improve the quality of wood for products. Forest tree pruning was also done to maintain the quality of fast-growing trees that were planted far apart. When trees are planted far apart, they grow faster, but lower branches stay alive longer. The large lower branches had to be pruned.

Bonsai was done to regulate size and shape to an extreme.

Now, when a house developer carves homesites into a forest, the homeowner wants trees in the garden, fruit trees behind the house, a bonsai on the patio, a windbreak of forest trees, and fast growing trees near the house and power lines.

THE CONFUSION STARTS

The homeowner remembers seeing pollarding and topiary in pruning books. Why not do the same to the forest trees and the fruit trees? If small trees can be topped why not big trees? Then the big trees get mutilated. But the mutilation is called pollarding. The fruit trees and flowering trees get sheared and "rounded over" by pruning them as if they were shrubs or rose bushes.

The point. There have been very few, if any, tree pruning books that discuss pruning from the view of tree health first. People have seen too many books where trees are discussed along with shrubs, roses, and raspberries.

Another reason. For centuries people were told how to take branches off trees. It was not until 1985 that a scientific paper was published by the author that explained how branches were attached to trees. As a result of this research, we now have a better understanding of the anatomy of branch attachment, and of the natural defense system in the base of the branch.

The point. Once you understand branch anatomy, you will know how to remove a branch properly.

Next reason. People knew that pruning caused wounds. And, wounds should "heal". "Callus" woundwood—was considered a sign of wound "healing". The larger the pruning wound, the larger the "callus". The larger the wound, the larger the column of rot in the tree. But, now that they knew how to "heal" wounds, it was the responsibility of others to find a wound dressing to stop the rot. That dressing has not yet come.

And last. People think that because trees are so big and tough you can do anything to them and they will stay alive. There is still great confusion over what a tree will *tolerate* and what is beneficial for the tree. Some trees such as London plane, linden or lime, and willows will tolerate mutilation. This does not mean it is good for them.

The point. It is time to focus on tree health first. A healthy tree will provide much, for many, for a long time.

DR. HANS MAYER-WEGELIN and THE HISTORY OF PRUNING

In 1936, Dr. Mayer-Wegelin published an excellent book on pruning (Mayer-Wegelin, H. 1936, Astung. M. & H. Schaper, Hannover).

The book outlines the different periods of pruning in Europe. The book explains the branch protection zone and the controversies on how to make the pruning cut. I am including here only a few excerpts. People who are really interested in pruning will find this book of extreme value. An English translation is in the United States Forest Service Library as Translation 364.

EXCERPTS

In the past German foresters twice have had recourse to pruning to a large extent, at first in the 18th century and then in the last third of the 19th century. Twice a period of intense pruning was followed by a reactionary period, a more or less prolonged period, during which pruning fell into disrepute and oblivion.

Pruning, however, in the 18th century was no innovation. It was prescribed in the various forest ordinances of the 16th century, mentioned in "Hausvater" literature and discussed in Carlowitz's "Wilde Baumzucht" (Wild Silviculture). In France and Belgium pruning was highly developed as a specialty of a separate craft guild.

Not only was there a good deal of pruning but "never had pruning been done so badly as in those days".

For many subsequent decades there prevailed among foresters an intense distrust of pruning in general.

In this respect the treatise on pruning by De Courval opened up new ways. Instead of the old removal procedure of stumping the branches of oak trees, a method that led to the rotting of the stems, he introduced a new procedure of removing the branches smoothly and closely to the stem and protecting the wounds immediately by putting on a thick layer of tar.

In forest literature there has been considerable dispute as to whether pruning should occur in front of the swelling or through it.

In the base of the dead hardwood branch the dead wood is almost always clearly separated from the living wood which is nourished laterally from the stem. "A dark, narrow strip indicates the boundary." "A cross section through the base of a dead beech branch clearly shows a definitely defined, narrow, reddish-brown separating layer between the outer dead part and the inner portion of the branch which is still full of sap and green."

This dark colored zone is a protective area in which tyloses are formed and the wound gum substances are deposited. The tree envelopes the dead branch and thus protects itself against disturbances in the activity of the living wood.

In a manner similar to beech other hardwoods also form a pronounced protective layer at the base of the branch.

The formation of the protective layer begins in the cambium of the branch and penetrates from the outside toward the pith. It depends on the presence of living cells.

Conifers, too, form at the base of dead branches a special protective layer by resin accumulation.

For, when the history of pruning teaches us that in spite of its repeated introduction and the experience gained from a century's forestry practice, pruning was not accepted in improvement measures, the reason being the fact that many of the prunings had brought about a diminution and not an increase in timber value.

One question has been discussed frequently in pruning literature, namely, whether the pruning cut should occur through the swelling at the branch base or immediately above it. After Büchting had made the demand in 1756 that the branch should be cut "just above the curled ring", the question has been touched upon in many publications. Almost all of the numerous authors decided in favor of sawing through the branch swelling and base this on the fact that the wound heals over more rapidly when the cut goes through the swelling, even if the wounded surface itself is larger than when the cut occurs above the swelling.

When green pruning of suppressed branches which already show a pronounced swelling at their bases takes place, a cut through the swelling makes a more rapid healing possible. A detailed explanation of this fact we owe to Kienitz.

Therefore, to bring about as early a healing as possible the most practical cut should go through the swelling at the base of the branch. In literature this pruning regulation is supplemented by another requirement, namely, that the pruning cut should be made close to the stem but not too close, that is, "just above the annual ring around the base of the branch."

The wound made by pruning as close as possible to the stem surface heals over most quickly.

In 1756 Büchting said that the branch collar should not be injured or removed. Many tree workers have said the same words for centuries. Yet, the collars were cut and the protection zones were destroyed. Why? Because large "callus"— woundwood—ribs were considered a sign of healing. And, that wood is dead. And, wound dressings will stop rot. These problems are still with us today.

DR. ROBERT HARTIG AND PRUNING

Dr. Robert Hartig is considered by many to be the father of forest pathology. Dr. Hartig considered Dr. Moritz Willkomm as the father of forest pathology (Willkomm, M. 1866. Die Mikroskopischen Feinde des Waldes. G. Schonfeld's Buchhandlung (C.A. Werner), Dresden]. Willkomm's book is one of the best early books on tree diseases. The only problem was that Willkomm believed that decay caused fungi. After the work of DeBary and others, Hartig showed that fungi caused decay (Hartig, R. 1878. Die Zersetzungserscheinungen Des Holzes. Verlag von Julius Springer, Berlin).

Even if you do not read German, the last three plates in Hartig's book are easy to understand. He has drawings in plates 19, 20, and 21 that show the branch protection zone clearly. He shows the zone after a dead branch has fallen. He shows the insides of trunks that received proper and improper cuts. A ring of wound-wood circles the proper cut.

My point, again, is that all of this was well known many years ago. Indeed, there is little new under the sun.

It is sad when we consider that centuries of sound research by many fine researchers has been blocked by the perpetuation of *three foolish myths: callus means healing, wood is dead, and wound dressings stop rot.*

I was very pleased to see a recent publication by Professor Dr. Walter Liese and associates (Liese, W., D. Dujesiefken, and J. Bremer. 1988. Wundreaktion bei Linde nach Astung in der Baumpflege, Forstw. Cbl. 107, 184-196). The last line of the English summary states, "These results on lime trees are concordant with observations by Shigo on North American hardwoods that a flush cut causes higher damage to the tree than cutting a branch above its collar." Maybe this will help to bring us back to Büchting who said the same words in 1756. Science advances more on rediscovery than discovery.

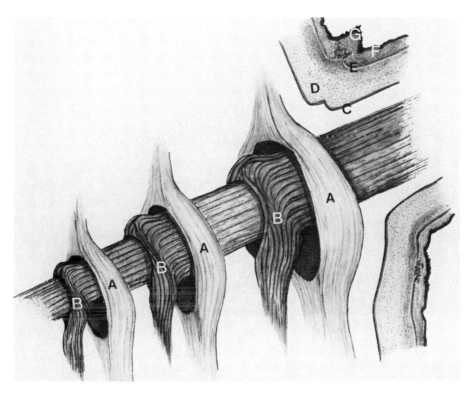

BRANCH ANATOMY

Three growth rings are pulled apart in the diagram to show the trunk collars (A) and branch collars (B).

Other features shown are: cambial zone (C), inner bark or phloem (D), bark cambium (E), outer corky bark (F), and the branch bark ridge (G).

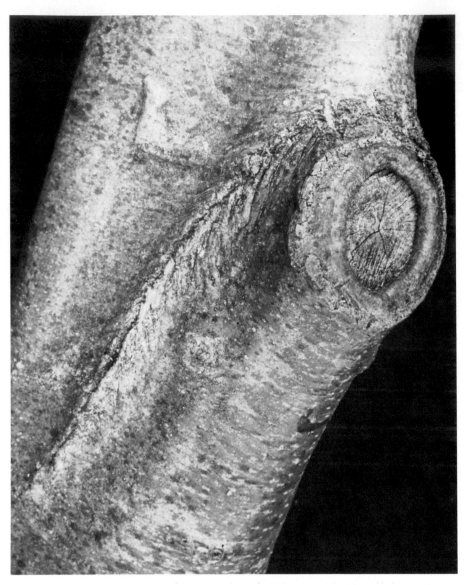

WOUNDWOOD AFTER PROPER CUT

When pruning cuts are made properly, a circle of woundwood will form the next growing season.

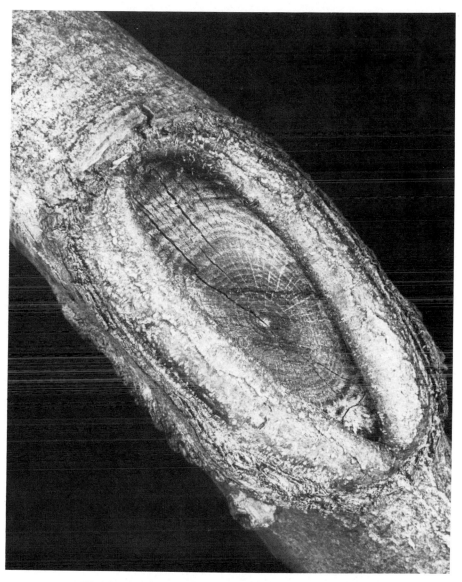

WOUNDWOOD AFTER IMPROPER CUT

When pruning cuts are made improperly, woundwood may form only to the sides of the wound, or partially about the wound.

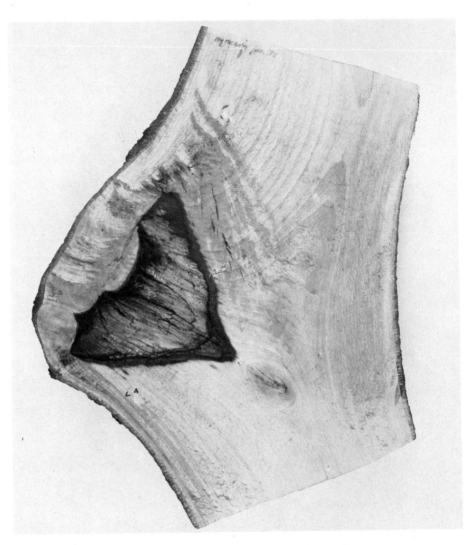

BRANCH PROTECTION ZONE

A 9-year-old proper pruning cut on a European beech from Holland (Courtesy, R. B. L. DeDorschkamp, Wageningen).

The wood within the cone-shaped protection zone was completely decayed. The wound was closed. The decay process was ended.

A boundary of discolored wood separated the decayed wood from the sound wood.

Treatments that break the natural boundaries destroy one of the tree's most important protection systems.

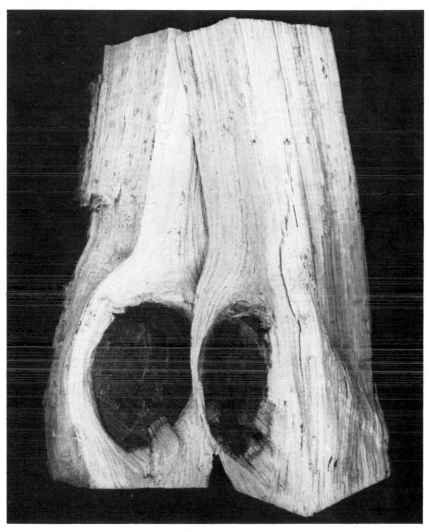

LARGE PRUNING CUTS ON OLD TREES

Here is a 50-year-old closed and well compartmentalized pruning cut on a white oak from Iowa. A small amount of dieback occurred below the cut. When pruning large branches on old trees, some dieback may occur on the trunk below the branch. Wait until the woundwood shows the limits of the dieback and then remove the dead bark. Do not try to anticipate where the dieback will occur. On large branches, the trunk collar may not envelop completely the branch collar, and that is why the small area of dieback may develop.

Before the chainsaw, most pruning cuts were proper because a proper cut was the easiest cut to make with a handsaw.

155

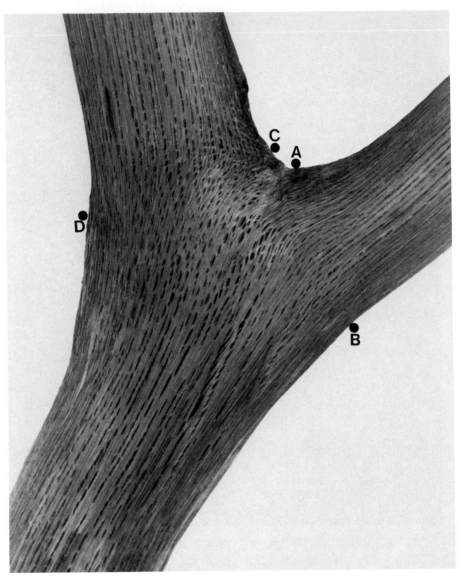

CODOMINANT STEM

The bark was removed on the red oak to show the union of codominant stems. There are no collars at the union of the stems. To remove the right stem, cut from B to A, and to remove the left stem, cut from D to C.

TRUNK COLLAR

The trunk collar envelops the branch collar on the red oak sample. To remove the branch, cut as close as possible to the collar.

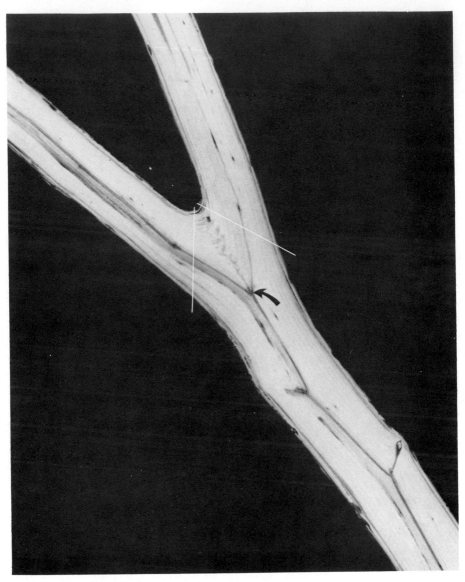

CODOMINANT STEMS ON AMERICAN ELM

1. The arrow shows the origin of two codominant stems. Note the U-shaped crotch that indicates a strong union. The proper cut lines are shown for each stem.

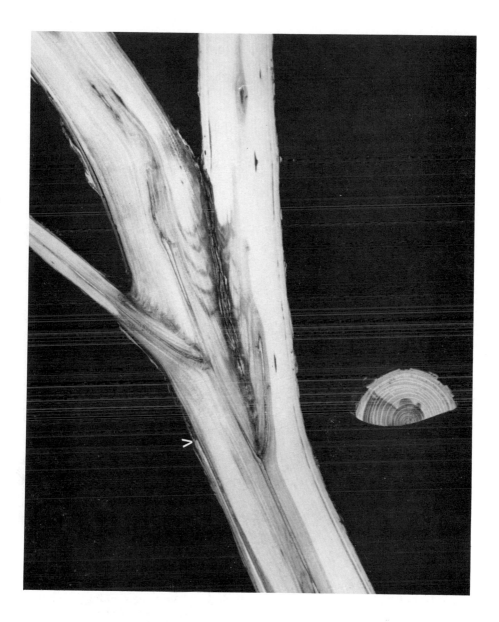

2. The codominant stems have included bark between them. As the stems
squeezed together, the wood on the inner sides of the stems discolored and died.
The stem at left died from infection by *Ophiostoma ulmi*, the fungus that causes
Dutch elm disease. The infection stayed on the left side of the trunk below the
union of the stems. Pathogens do not spread from one codominant stem to the
other. The pointer shows where the downward spread of the pathogen stopped.
Only one narrow growth ring separates the infected wood from the cambium.

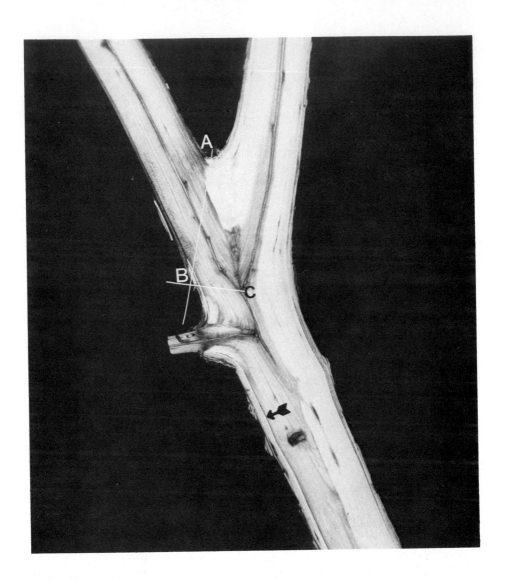

3. An infected codominant stem is at left and a healthy stem at right. This photo is similar to figure 2, except there is no included bark between the stems. A proper cut would be from A to B. The union of the stems is at C. Point A is close to the stem bark ridge within the crotch of the stems. Point B is where a straight line is drawn from the bottom of the stem bark ridge, which is the same as point C. The arrow shows the narrow growth ring of healthy wood. The pathogen was stopped at point B. The thin band of healthy wood was the wood that formed after the pathogen was stopped at point B. The pathogen did not spread to the right of the trunk.

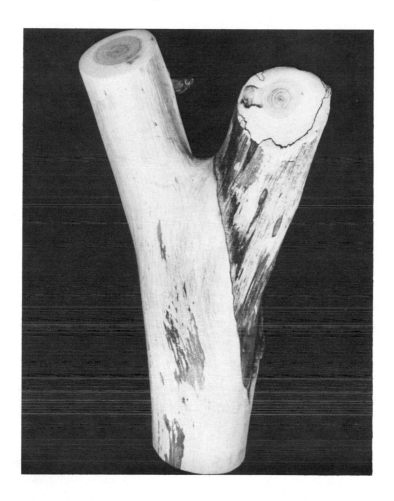

4. Note the clear, healthy wood in the living stem. The microorganisms in the dead stem did not spread to the living stem at left.

The purpose of showing these photos of American elm is to reinforce the point that pathogens do not spread at will in trees. If proper pruning cuts are made on infected branches or codominant stems on elms or oaks, the pathogen will stay in those tissues connected with the stem or branch. The worst that could happen from a healthy branch that was pruned properly would be the infection of a small strip of wood on the trunk below the branch.

The real damage to oaks infected with the fungus that causes oak wilt and to elms infected with the fungus that causes Dutch elm disease, results when flush cuts are made. And, to make the injury even worse, climbing spikes are often used during pruning. Then, a wound dressing is applied to hide the injuries!

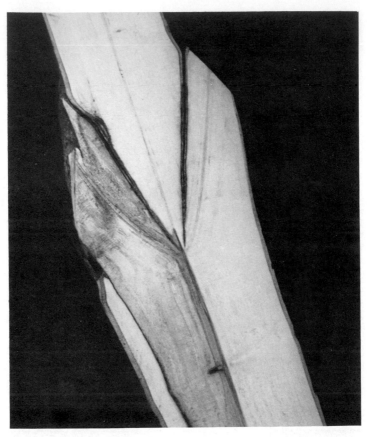

PROPER PRUNING OF A BRANCH WITH INCLUDED BARK

The branch at left was pruned 2 years before the tree was cut. Note the included bark between the branch and the trunk. The cambium died back slightly below the cut. The infection developed only downward within the tissues present at the time of the pruning cut. Healthy tissues formed after the cut was made.

At right is a proper cut made at the time the red maple tree was cut. When removing a branch with included bark always stub cut the branch first. Then cut upward to remove the stub. Do not injure the trunk above the branch. No matter how a branch with included bark is cut, the top portion of the branch core is the same as a protruding stub. Callus and woundwood will form on the lower portion of the cut but seldom on the upper portion.

Branches with included bark are often embedded deeply within the trunk. Try to make cuts that remove the branch but do not injure the trunk.

INTERMITTENT INCLUDED BARK

Included bark forms when the cambium of the branch and the trunk turn inward within the branch crotch. Some branches have included bark when they begin to develop.

The arrow shows where the included bark ended on the inner portion of the branch on this Canadian hemlock. The growth rings turned outward above the arrow. Included bark may be strongly regulated by genetics, but other factors must also be involved or we would not find branches that grow in or out of included bark.

I believe that included bark forms when the branch and trunk grow at the same time. In the forest, the branch usually grows before the trunk. When we bring trees into our world, we change their pattern of growth, and the entire tree grows at the same time.

CALLUS AND WOUNDWOOD

Wounds are injuries to living tissues that are usually inflicted suddenly.

After wounds injure wood in living trees, a long series of physiological and anatomical events take place. The first response is an electrical one. Then chemical changes take place. Stored energy reserves in living parenchyma cells are converted through long biochemical pathways to substances that are inhibitory to most wood-inhabiting microorganisms. The substances form a boundary that resists the spread of microorganisms into the wood. The boundary also defends the liquid transport, energy storage, and mechanical support systems of the tree. This boundary is called the reaction zone.

When the cambial zone about the wound resumes growth, the newly formed cells differentiate to form a boundary that separates the wood present at the time of injury from new wood that will form after the boundary is completed. That separating boundary is called the barrier zone.

On the margin of the wound, the cambial zone produces large, undifferentiated, nonlignified, homogeneous cells called callus. As callus production continues, some of the cells begin to differentiate to form transport cells — vessels, tracheids — and fibers. When these cells become lignified, then we have woundwood. The woundwood expands as ribs or rolls about the wound because there is no pressure to confine the growing cells.

In 1925 Professor Dr. E. Küster at the Botanical Institute of the University of Halle wrote a large detailed book on pathological plant anatomy (Küster, E. 1925. Pathologische Pflanzenanatomie, Fisher, Jena, 558 pp.). In the book he describes in great detail the changes that take place after wounding. He makes strong points for the differences between callus and woundwood, and also woundcork. People interested in details should read the book. An English translation is available in the library of the United States Forest Service Laboratory at Hamden, Connecticut.

CRACKS, WETWOOD, and BRANCH FAILURE

Cracks are major starting points for trunk and branch failures. Wounds are major starting points for cracks.

Wetwood often develops along the cracks. Wetwood is caused by bacteria that can live where there is little or no free oxygen. The bacteria digest and alter cell contents and the materials between cells. As a result of these actions, the infected wood is high in moisture, microelements, and pH. But, because of the changes in the infected wood, wood-decaying fungi usually are not able to infect the wetwood. So, in a sense, wetwood is a biological protection wood.

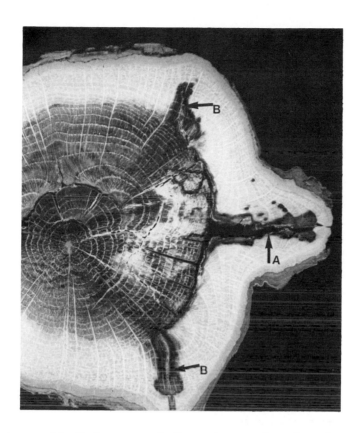

Wounds caused by flush cuts are similar to the wound on the red oak trunk in the photo. The ribs of woundwood may eventually close the wound. Crack A is called the primary crack. As the first few ribs of woundwood roll inward at the margins of the wound, secondary cracks may develop (B). The secondary cracks start from the inside and may spread outward. Wetwood often develops along the secondary cracks. When the cracks are on large lateral branches, the secondary cracks may spread outward and break through the bark.

As the secondary cracks spread outward, the branch becomes similar to two cantilevered beams; one on top and the other on the bottom. So long as the wetwood along the secondary cracks keeps the wood moist, the branch will bend. When the cracks begin to dry, the branch may fracture.

Branches fail in two basic ways: loading beyond the resisting strength of the wood, or increasing the weakening of some defective portion of the branch. When a weak spot gets weaker, a branch may fail even when no additional loading occurs. Any branch will fail when loading exceeds the strength of the branch — wind, snow, ice, rain, or abundance of growth. The important point here is to understand that as secondary cracks that have wetwood begin to dry, the branch may fail when there is no additional loading.

CLADOPTOSIS

Twigs and branches are shed normally on many species of trees. This shedding process is called cladoptosis. A corky layer forms at the base of the twigs or branches. The tree shown here is a Brachychyton from Australia. It sheds large branches.

Some people become concerned when they see many twigs or small branches falling from their trees. Consult a professional to learn whether this is a normal process of your tree.

TOOLS

The first pruning tools were heavy knives and axes. Pruning was also done by beating dead and dying branches off the trees with clubs. Now we have a great variety of pruning tools: shears operated by compressed air, hydraulic devices, propane-powered shears, chainsaws, rotary blades, and an endless variety of other tools. Most were designed to make what was considered a proper cut — a flush cut. Indeed, it is time for some new tools.

Here are two tools used by the people who practice bonsai. The one at left makes a cut from the side. The other is called a "melon ball cutter". The tool at left often leaves a stub. The tool at right often cuts too deeply into the trunk. A tool is only as good as the user. Care must be taken so as not to leave stubs or to remove the protection zone. It is too easy to over cut. Yet, when used properly, these are fine tools. As always, look for the circle of woundwood. Then you know the cut was proper.

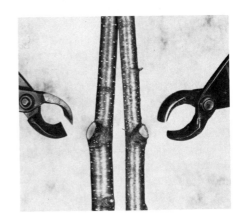

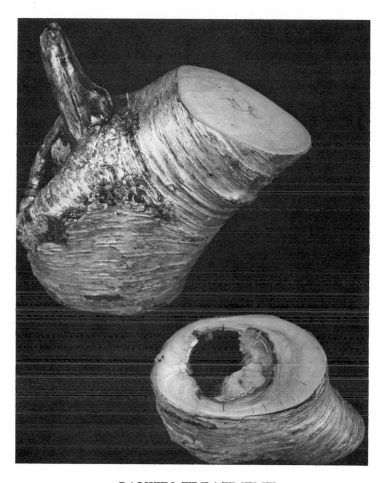

CAVITY TREATMENT

Cavities often form after flush cuts or stub cuts. The photo shows the top and bottom of the same sample. The cavity formed where there was a stub left on a codominant stem.

If a cavity fills with water, do not drill holes to drain the water. The holes will break the boundary that walls off the decay. If some treatment is wanted, siphon out the water, clean away the decay, and fill with an expandable foam. When cleaning the cavity, do not injure or break the boundary that walls off the decay. There is no way to sterilize wood and keep it sterile. Do not injure or remove the wound-wood when cleaning a cavity. No amount of wound dressing will replace the natural protection features of a tree.

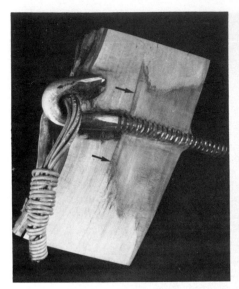 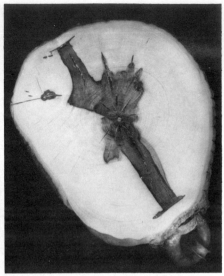

CABLING AND BRACING

Branches with weak unions can be strengthened by proper installation of cables and braces by professionals.

Screw lags (left) can be used on small branches where there is no decay. The arrows show the size of the stem at the time of treatment. Long-term holding by a cable is provided by the wood that forms after installation. When using lag screws with open ends, do not turn the open ends into the bark.

On large branches or on branches that have some internal defects, use steel rods or bolts that go through the stem. Place round washers and nuts on both sides, (right). Seat the round washers on the wood, or countersink them so they will be flat against the wood. Do not place them deep into the wood or on the surface of the bark.

Never tie branches together with wire or ropes.

Always check cables and braces to see that they are safe. Look for dead spots and cracks near the insertion holes. If problems start, remove the branch.

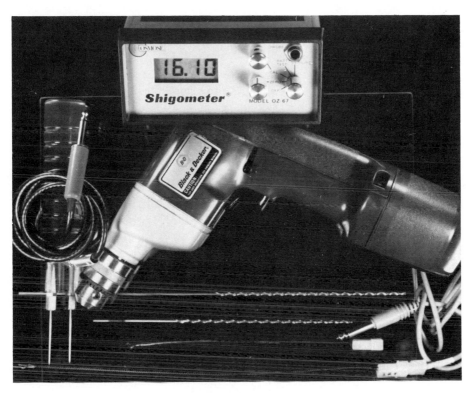

SHIGOMETRY

Decay in roots, trunks, and branches can be detected accurately by shigometry. There are several devices now being used that have the same operating principle. A small hole, 2 to 3 mm. in diameter is drilled into the trunk. A special electrode is inserted slowly into the hole. The electrode is attached to a meter that generates a pulsed-electric current and measures the resistance to the current in ohms. As the tip of the electrode contacts wood along the hole, the electrical resistance is shown on the face of the meter. Abrupt decreases in resistance usually indicate decay. To use the method properly a sound understanding of compartmentalization is needed. The method takes practice and skill. It is not easy. But, once learned, a great amount of information can be obtained.

The small hole made by the drill bit does break boundaries, but the hole is so small that the tree usually walls off the injured tissues rapidly. The small injury must be weighed against the information that can be gained.

Needle electrodes can be used to determine the vitality of the tree.

CODIT

CODIT is a model of compartmentalization. CODIT is an acronym for Compartmentalization **Of Decay In Trees.**

Compartmentalization is the tree defense process where boundaries form that resist spread of pathogens. The boundaries also defend the liquid transport, energy storage, and mechanical support systems. So long as boundaries limit infections to small volumes of wood, large volumes of wood will remain active for liquid transport, energy storage, and mechanical support.

Compartmentalization is a two part process: first a boundary forms within the wood present at the time of injury and infection — reaction zone — and then a boundary forms from new cells that separate the wood present at the time of injury from cells that continue to form after the boundary is completed — barrier zone.

CODIT also has two parts: Part 1 is represented by walls 1, 2, and 3. The walls serve to give the reaction zone three dimensions. Part 2: wall 4 is a model representation of the barrier zone.

Walls 1, 2, and 3 are model representations of the reaction zone. Wall 1 represents all the factors that resist vertical spread above and below the wound. Vessels and tracheids can be plugged in many ways: gums, granular materials, tyloses, pit closure, embolisms, microorganisms. Wall 2 represents all the factors that resist inward spread of infections. Wall 3 represents all factors that resist lateral spread of infections. Wall 1 is usually the weakest and wall 3 is the strongest in Part 1.

Wall 4 is even stronger than wall 3. In some trees, the barrier zone has been shown to contain suberin, which is the material that makes cork resistant to breakdown by microorganisms.

The photo at right shows a red maple with a 2-year-old pruning cut that removed the protection zone at right, and a larger but more shallow wound of the same age at left. The numbers refer to the CODIT walls. The photo also shows that a large shallow wound causes less injury than a wound that removes the branch protection zone.

Some individuals of a species form boundaries that are stronger than other individuals of the same species.

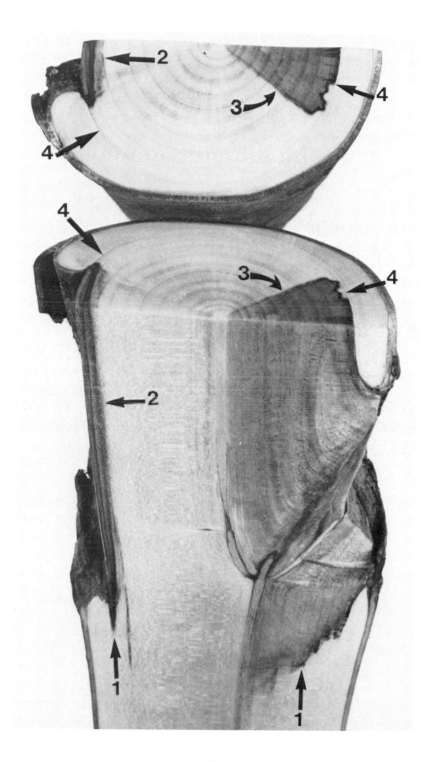

13

Questions you need to ask. Discuss the results with a
tree professional — arborist.

You could help your trees, and save a life: maybe yours!

1. TARGET
If the tree falls will it hit cars, houses, power lines or people?

2. ARCHITECTURE
Has the tree grown beyond its normal form into a dangerous form?

3. HISTORY
Has the tree lost branches recently?

4. EDGE TREE
Were neighboring trees cut away recently leaving tall trees at the edge?

5. DEAD BRANCHES
Are there dead tops or branches?
Is the tree dead?

6. CRACKS
Are there deep, open cracks in the trunk and branches?

7. CROTCH CRACKS
Are there deep, open cracks below joining stems?

8. LIVING BRANCHES

Do living branches bend abruptly upward or downward where tips of large branches were cut off—tipping?

9. TOPPING

Are large branches growing rapidly from topping cuts on big trees?

10. STORM INJURY

Are there broken branches, split trunks, or injured roots?
Are branches close to power lines?

11. ROOT ROT

Are there fungus fruit bodies—mushrooms—on roots?
Were roots injured by construction?

12. ROTS AND CANKERS

Are there hollows or cankers—dead spots—any with fungus fruit bodies?
Is the tree leaning?

13. CONSTRUCTION INJURY

Have roots, trunk, or branches been injured?
Is there a new lawn or garden over injured roots?

WARNING!

Hazardous trees are very unpredictable. If you think you have a tree problem, discuss it with a tree professional — arborist.

Do not try to remedy the problem yourself.

To remedy a problem it may be necessary to remove the target, remove parts of the tree or the entire tree, or cable and brace the weak parts of the tree. Again, these are jobs only for trained arborists who are insured!

Work with arborists to keep your trees beautiful, healthy and
HAZARD FREE

PROPER PLANTING AND PRUNING

Proper pruning is one of the most important treatments for a tree after it is planted properly. Here are some important points on proper planting.

Know what kind of tree you want.

Know what type of planting site you have.

Get advice from professionals on the best trees for your site.

Is your planting site sunny (A) or shady (B) wet (C) or dry (D)?

Is your soil sandy or loose (E) or compact and heavy (F)?

Is your pH high or low (G)?

Remove injured and dying roots (H) and injured and dying branches (J). *Do not remove living branches in attempts to balance top growth with the amount of roots.*

Prepare a planting site (K, L) not just a small hole. Loosen the soil far beyond the soil that will hold the tree (K).

Do not amend the soil with anything, unless the planting site has very poor soil or consists of building rubble. If amendments are used, incorporate the materials into the planting site.

If you have a choice, it is better to plant a tree where water must be added rather than where water must be drained away. On very wet sites or on sites that have heavy clays, the tree could be planted on a mound. The mound should be at least 3 meters in diameter and a half meter high in the center. In preparing the mound, the parent soil below the mound must be loosened and mixed with the soil of the mound.

A small covering of well-composted chips or other mulch materials may be placed round the base of the tree (M). Do not use large amounts of fresh wood chips. Water well beyond the base of the tree (N).

Fertilize lightly after the leaves have formed. Always water when you fertilize.

Do not put fertilizer in the soil at the time of planting.

Keep flowers, weeds, (P) and grass (Q) away from the base of the tree.

If the tree is not firm in the soil, brace in a way that allows the trunk to move slightly. Brace as low on the trunk as possible to provide stability for the tree.

Do not use wire in a hose. Do not put nails or screws into the trunk. Use flat strapping that will not injure the bark. Remove the braces when the tree becomes established, usually a year or two at the most.

Tree wrappings are mainly cosmetic. Do not buy a tree that has the trunk wrapped.

Start pruning the tree after the leaves form to establish the framework you want (S). Keep pruning, during the *proper* time periods, to maintain the framework.

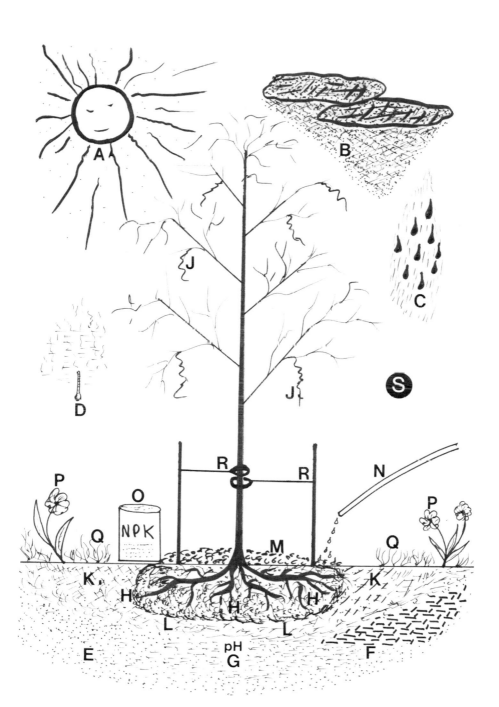

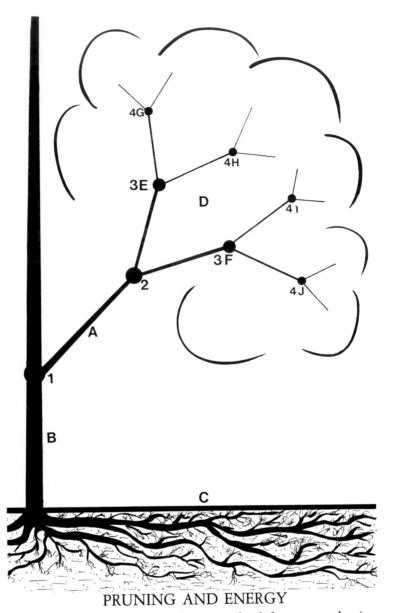

PRUNING AND ENERGY

Leaves or needles on D must provide energy for defense, reproduction and all the living cells in the wood and inner bark of A, B, C, and D.

On young, small trees one branch may be removed from each of positions 4G, H, I, J, or from 3E or F, or from 2. Or the entire branch removed at 1.

As trees grow older and A, B, and C get larger, the amount of living wood removed from D should decrease. On mature and over-mature trees, only dead, dying, diseased and hazardous branches should be removed. If many sprouts grow after pruning, D has been over pruned.

PRUNING AND FERTILIZING, AND PHENOLOGY

Phenology is the study of periodic natural phenomena, or the timing of natural processes. Trees have 5 major phenological periods: (1) onset of growth; (2) formation of leaves or needles; (3) formation of wood and inner bark; (4) storage of energy; and (5) dormancy.

Organisms associated with trees also have phenological periods: (1) onset of growth; (2) maturation; (3) reproduction; (4) migration to new habitats or expansion of old habitats; (5) resting stage. Some of the tree associates are beneficial to the tree and some are potentially destructive. Some of the micro-associates may complete the 5 stages in minutes when conditions are proper for them. Most destructive associates are most active during tree periods 1, and between 4 and 5.

The periods are like themes. There are many variations on the themes. The periods are affected greatly by environmental factors. Trees in cold climates will have different phenological patterns from trees in hot climates.

Let us look more closely at the 5 tree periods.

Period 1 is the time when nonwoody roots, mycorrhizae mostly, are absorbing water and elements (not food) from the soil. Nitrogen and all other elements that enter the tree must be in a soluble inorganic form. Organic molecules contain carbon, and usually the carbon is bonded to hydrogen and oxygen. Inorganic molecules do not contain carbon. When organic substances are added to the soil, the microorganisms alter the substances and inorganic soluble substances are the results. When nitrogen enters the tree in an inorganic form, most of the nitrogen combines with carbohydrates to form amino acids. Amino acids are building blocks for protoplasm. The end result is more tissue.

Period 2 is the time leaves and needles (henceforth called leaves) are forming. As leaves are forming from buds that formed the previous year, new buds are forming in the axils of the leaves or at tips in some conifers.

Period 3 is the time wood and inner bark are forming. Some trees form flowers and fruit in periods 2 and 3. Fruit on many trees begin to mature in period 4.

Period 4 is the time energy reserves as starch and fats are being deposited in living cells in sapwood. Some reproductive parts begin to form in period 4. The male cones and strobili form and they will be ready to produce pollen at the end of period 1 the next year. The current increment of wood begins to store starch and fats during the latter part of period 4.

Period 5 is the time leaves are shedding. Nonwoody roots begin to shed near the end of period 4 and they continue to shed during the beginning of period 5. As the old nonwoody roots are shedding, new nonwoody roots are forming. The fungi that are the associates of the nonwoody roots usually produce sporophores or mushrooms during the beginning of period 5. In cold climates, the growth of nonwoody roots slows during the middle of period 5. The nonwoody roots begin to grow again at end of period 5.

Growth of nonwoody roots in period 5 and the functioning of the nonwoody roots in period 1 are driven by energy stored in living cells in the woody roots. The formation of leaves and new buds, and flowers in some species, in period 1 are also powered mostly by stored energy.

When the leaves are fully formed, photosynthate produced by them drives the processes that form xylem and phloem. When the xylem is lignified, it becomes wood. Most of the wood and phloem are formed in 6 to 8 weeks after the leaves have fully formed.

As period 5 starts, the electrical resistance of the cambial zone and wood increase indicating a change in the electrical state of the tree as it goes into dormancy. The increase in electrical resistance can be detected by using the Shigometer. Two needle electrodes are forced into the inner bark and wood. A pulsed-electric current passes from the Shigometer into one needle electrode, through the tissues, back through the other needle, and to an ohmmeter in the Shigometer.

It is important to know the phenological periods of the trees you are pruning and fertilizing. It is also important to know the phenological periods of the potential pathogens.

When you prune and fertilize, you are affecting the tree *and* its associates. Care must be taken to do the treatments in a way and at a time that will benefit the trees and not the pathogens.

Now comes the difficult part: how much to prune and fertilize and when to do the treatments. When you prune, you are making wounds where pathogens could infect. When you remove living tissue, you are removing leaves that provide energy for the tree. When you fertilize, you are providing elements for the pathogens in the soil as well as for the tree. When you provide high amounts of soluble nitrogen at a time when there are no leaves on the tree, the amino acids will form from stored energy reserves. When stored energy reserves are lowered, defense is lowered. And when defense is lowered pathogens usually attack.

On healthy, young trees the best time to make training cuts is during periods 3 and 5. Trees could be fertilized to have nitrogen and other elements available during periods 1, 2, 3, and the beginning of 4. Care must be taken not to stimulate growth into the latter part of period 4 in cold climates.

On older healthy trees, remove diseased, dying, and hazardous branches anytime. Period 5 is a good time to remove dead branches.

A tree is mature when the dynamic mass to energy ration is 1 to 1. On mature and over mature trees, remove only diseased, dying, dead, and hazardous branches.

Healthy mature trees can be fertilized to have nitrogen and other elements available during periods 1, 2, 3, and the beginning of 4. As trees begin to reach maturity, the amount of nitrogen provided for them should be reduced.

On stressed trees—low energy reserves—diseased trees, and trees injured by construction, remove diseased, dying, dead, and hazardous living branches only. Do not remove healthy living branches. Do not remove healthy living branches in attempts to "balance" the amount of roots removed during construction. Wait until the tree branches begin to die. Then remove them. Do not try to anticipate which branches will die or you might remove the healthy branches that will support the tree. On many trees, the roots are in line with branches. But, the tissues often spiral on a trunk and the root on one side may be in line with branches on the opposite side of the tree.

After construction injury, protect the tree from further injuries and keep the tree watered. Add dilute amounts of fertilizers to make nitrogen available during periods 3 and 4. Several treatments with dilute amounts of fertilizers could be done during periods 3 and 4. Use great care not to have high amounts of nitrogen available during periods 1 and 2. The nitrogen will bond with carbohydrate to form more and larger twigs and leaves. The added nitrogen may stimulate the growth of dormant buds. When reserve carbohydrate is lowered, defense is lowered. After the tree regains health, the fertilizer schedule for healthy trees can be started.

When large woody roots are injured, use care in adding fertilizers that will make high amounts of nitrogen available for the pathogens in the soil that rot roots. Be especially careful where trees are growing in hot climates. Periods 2, 4 and 5 are the times when many of the root pathogens are most active.

The information given here should be used as a guide. There will always be exceptions to the guidelines given. Environmental conditions at the times of pruning and fertilizing will also play a major role in whether the treatments are beneficial or not.

The best procedure is to watch the tree after the treatments are done. Watch for signs of mistreatment: excessive growth of sprouts, insect borers, early leaf fall, dying twigs, many scale insects, abnormally large leaves, increase in cambial electrical resistance, and loss of stored starch in living cells as shown by iodine in potassium iodide (I_2-KI).

Keep a safety check as well as a health check on the tree. If your treatment amounts and times are benefitting the tree, keep doing what you have done. And remember the phenological times when you did the treatments so you can repeat them later.

If the treatment amounts and times seem to be more harmful than helpful, try changing the amounts and timing. But, still remember what the "bad" times and amounts were so you *do not* repeat them.

The better we understand the tree and the many factors that affect the tree, the better we can treat the tree to be healthy, attractive, and hazard free.

POSTLUDE

Pruning will always be a controversial subject because it includes so many variables: how to prune, how much to prune, what to prune, when to prune, how often to prune, how to prune trees that have different tolerances to pruning, how to prune trees as they age, how to prune for fruit, espalier, topiary, pleaching, pollarding, bonsai, biomass, quality timber, windbreaks, shade, sun; and the list goes on.

The answer is simple. Learn how trees are constructed, how they function, and how they defend themselves. Then, you can prune to help the trees and their associates and to get what you want from the tree. Unless this is done, the controversies will continue.

Pruning brings together science, art, and common sense. Science gives us information about the tree. Art is the skill or ability to bring about a desired result. Common sense means the use of good judgement in doing something and remembering the result. When you do something that gives what you want, you remember what you did and you do it again. If what you did resulted in something you did not want, you do not repeat it. Right? Wrong!

Look at all the tree mutilation that is repeated. Where is the common sense?

People without common sense want rule books. There will always be someone to sell them such a book.

I believe that people who really love trees will learn about them. Love means understanding.

Sad, but true, some people do not like trees. And, there are other people who see trees only as another source of profit. They are quick to sell many magic cures. That is the history of wound dressings and Dutch elm disease.

Please, let me end with an excerpt from one of my favorite books, "Sarton on the history of science", by George Sarton, 1962, Harvard University Press, Cambridge, Massachusetts, page 134. Here he is discussing two of my heroes, Andreas Vesalius and Leonardo Da Vinci: "It is almost certain that he (Da Vinci) dissected more bodies than the professors of anatomy before his time; for not only were university dissections few and far between, but the professors did not lower themselves to that kind of dirty work. The dissection was generally made by an underling under the eyes of the professor who was sitting in his cathedra holding the textbook before him and giving occasional directions to the prosector. It was very difficult for the professor to see much from his high chair, and he was paying more attention to his book than to the cadaver."

In time, the medical professors put down their textbooks,
climbed down from their high chairs,
and touched the body.
That was the beginning of modern medicine.

It is time to do the same for trees.

It is time to start modern arboriculture.

CURIOSITY IS THE FUEL THAT POWERS
THE MACHINERY OF PROGRESS.
HUMOR IS THE LUBRICANT.

REFERENCES

The concepts in this guide are based on what I have done for 30 years with the help of many hard-working assistants and colleagues. Listed here in chronological order are 101 of the 270 publications that discuss the research. For a more complete list of references see *A New Tree Biology*, second edition.

PROFESSIONAL PAPERS AND PUBLICATIONS

1. Shigo, A.L. 1959. Fungi isolated from oak wilt trees and their effects on Ceratocystis fagacearum. Mycologia 50: 757-769.

2. Shigo, A.L. 1960. Parasitism of Gonatobotryum fuscum on species of Ceratocystis. Mycologia 53: 584-598.

3. Shigo, A.L., C.D. Anderson, and H.L. Barnett. 1961. Effects of concentration of host nutrients on parasitism of Piptocephalis xenophila and P. virginiana. Phytopathology 51: 616-620.

4. Shigo, A.L. 1962. Observations on the succession of fungi on hardwood pulpwood bolts. Plant Disease Reporter 46: 379-380.

5. Shigo, A.L. 1963. Fungi associated with the discoloration around rot columns caused by Fomes igniarius. Plant Disease Reporter 47: 820-823.

6. Shigo, A.L. 1964. Organism interactions in the beech bark disease. Phytopathology 54: 263-269.

7. Shigo, A.L. 1964. A canker on red maple caused by fungi infecting wounds made by the red squirrel. Plant Disease Reporter 48: 794-796.

8. Shigo, A.L. 1965. The pattern of decay and discoloration in northern hardwoods. Phytopathology 55: 648-652.

9. Shigo, A.L. 1965. Decay and discoloration in sprout red maple. Phytopathology 55: 957-962.

10. Shigo, A.L. 1966. Organism interaction to decay and discoloration in beech, birch, and maple. Mat. und Org., Duncker and Humbolt, Berlin. 309-324.

11. Shigo, A.L. 1967. Successions of organisms in discoloration and decay of wood. Inter. Rev. For. Res. 2. Academic Press. 65 p.

12. Shigo, A. L. and E. M. Sharon. 1968. Discoloration and decay in hardwoods following inoculations with Hymenomycetes. Phytopathology 58: 1493-1498.

13. Shigo, A. L. and E. vH Larson. 1969. A photo guide to the patterns of discoloration and decay in northern hardwood trees. USDA For. Serv. Res Pap. NE 127. NE For. Expt. Stn. 100 p.

14. Shigo, A. L. 1969. How the canker rot fungi, Poria obliqua and Polyporus glomeratus incite cankers. Phytopathology 59: 1164-1165.

15. Shigo, A. L. and E. M. Sharon. 1970. Mapping columns of discolored and decayed tissues in sugar maple, Acer saccharum Marsh. Phytopathology 60: 232-237.

16. Shigo, A. L. 1970. Growth of Polyporus glomeratus, Poria obliqua. Fomes igniarius, and Pholiota squarrose-adiposa in media amended with manganese, calcium, zinc, and iron. Mycologia 62: 604-607.

17. Cosenza, B. J., M. McCreary, J. D. Buck, and A. L. Shigo. 1970. Bacteria associated with discolored and decayed tissues in beech, birch, and maple. Phytopathology 60: 1547-1551.

18. Shigo, A. L., J. Stankewich, and B. J. Cosenza. 1971. Clostridium sp. associated with discolored tissues in living oaks. Phytopathology 61: 122-123.

19. Shigo, A. L. 1972. Successions of microorganisms and patterns of discoloration and decay after wounding in red oak and white oak. Phytopathology 62: 256-259.

20. Shigo, A. L. 1972. Ring and ray shakes associated with wounds in trees. Holzforschung 26: 60-62.

181

21. Shigo, A. L. 1972. The beech bark disease today in Northeastern United States. J. Forestry 70: 286-289.

22. Skutt, H. R., A. L. Shigo, and R. A. Lessard. 1972. Detection of discolored and decayed wood in living trees using a pulsed electric current. Can. J. For. Res. 2: 54-56.

23. Hepting, G. H. and A. L. Shigo. 1972. Difference in decay rate following fire between oaks in North Carolina and Maine. Plant Disease Reporter. 56: 406-407.

24. Tatter, T. A., A. L. Shigo, and T. Chase. 1972. Relationship between degree of resistance to pulsed electric current and wood in progressive stages of discoloration and decay in living trees. Can. J. For. Res. 2: 236-243.

25. Rier, J. P. and A. L. Shigo. 1972. Some changes in red maple, Acer rubrum, tissues within 34 days after wounding in July. Can. J. Bot. 50: 1783-1784.

26. Shigo, A. L. and W. E. Hillis. 1973. Heartwood, discolored wood, and microorganisms in living trees. Ann. Rev. Phytopathology 11: 197-222.

27. Shortle, W. C. and A. L. Shigo. 1973. Concentrations of manganese and microorganisms in discolored and decayed wood in sugar maple. Can. J. For. Res. 3: 354-358.

28. Shigo, A. L., W. B. Leak, and S. Filip. 1973. Sugar maple borer injury in four hardwood stands in New Hampshire. Can. J. For. Res. 3: 512-515.

29. Shigo, A. L. 1974. Effects of manganese, calcium, zinc, and iron on growth and pigmentation of Trichocladium canadense, Phialophora melinii, Hypoxylon rubiginosum, Daldinia concentrica, and Cystopora decipiens. Mycologia 66: 339-341.

30. Shigo, A. L. 1974. Relative abilities of Phialophora melinii, Fomes connatus, and F. igniarius to invade freshly wounded tissues of Acer rubrum. Phytopathology 64: 708-710.

31. Safford, L. O., A. L. Shigo, and M. Ashley. 1974. Concentrations of cations in discolored and decayed wood in red maple. Can. J. For. Res. 4: 435-440.

32. Sharon, E. M. and A. L. Shigo. 1974. A method for studying the relationship of wounding and microorganisms to the discoloration process in sugar maple. Can. J. For. Res. 4: 146-148.

33. Shigo, A. L. 1974. Biology of decay and wood quality. In Biological Transformation of Wood by Microorganisms. Walter Liese, Ed., Proc. Symposium. Wood Products Pathology. Springer-Verlag Co., Berlin, Heidelberg, New York 1975. 1-15.

34. McGinnes, E. A. and A. L. Shigo. 1975. Effects of wounds on heartwood formation in white oak. Wood and Fiber 5: 327-331.

35. Pottle, H. W. and A. L. Shigo. 1975. Treatment of wounds on Acer rubrum with Trichoderma viride. Eur. J. For. Pathol. 5: 274-279.

36. Shigo, A. L. and P. Berry. 1975. A new tool for detection of decay associated with Fomes annosus in Pinus resinosa. Plant Disease Reporter. 59: 739-742.

37. Shigo, A. L. 1975. Compartmentalization of decay associated with Fomes annosus in trunks of Pinus resinosa. Phytopathology 65: 1038-1039.

38. Shigo, A. L. 1975. Microorganisms associated with wounds inflicted during winter, summer, and fall in Acer rubrum, Betula papyrifera, Fagus grandifolia, and Quercus rubra. Phytopathology 66: 559-563.

39. Shigo, A. L. 1975. Compartmentalization of discolored and decayed wood in trees. Mat. und Org. Berlin, Belheft 3: 221-226.

40. Garrett, P. W., A. L. Shigo, and J. Carter. 1976. Variation in diameter of central columns of discoloration in six hybrid poplar clones. Can. J. For. Res. 6: 475-477.

41. Smith, D. E., A. L. Shigo, L. O. Safford, and R. Blanchard. 1976. Resistances to a pulsed electric current reveal differences between nonreleased, released, and released-fertilized paper birch trees. For. Sci. 22: 471-472.

42. Shigo, A. L. and C. L. Wilson. 1977. Wound dressings on red maple and American elm: Effectiveness after 5 years. J. Arboric. 3: 81-87.

43. Shigo, A. L., W. C. Shortle, and P. W. Garrett. 1977. Compartmentalization of discolored wood and decayed wood associated with injection-type wounds in hybrid poplar. J. Arboric. 3: 114-118.

44. Shigo, A. L., W. C. Shortle, and P. W. Garrett. 1977. Genetic control suggested in compartmentalization of discolored wood associated with tree wounds. For. Sci. 23: 179-182.

45. Shortle, W. C., A. L. Shigo, P. Berry, and J. Abusamra. 1977. Electrical resistance in tree cambium zone: Relationship to rates of growth and wound closure. For Sci. 23: 326-329.

46. Pottle, H. W., A. L. Shigo, and R. O. Blanchard. 1977. Biological control of wound hymenomycetes by Trichoderma harzianum. Plant Disease Reporter. 61: 687-690.

47. Shigo, A. L. 1977. Phialophora melinii: Effects of inoculations in wounded red maple. Phytopathology 67: 1333-1337.

48. Shigo, A. L., W. C. Shortle, and J. Ochrymowych. 1977. Shigometer method for detection of active decay at groundline in utility poles. Manual For. Serv. Gen. Tech. Rept. NE-35.

49. Shigo, A. L., N. Rogers, E. A. McGinnes, and D. Funk. 1978. Black walnut strip mine spoils: Some observations 25 years after pruning. USDA For. Serv. Res. Pap. NE-393. 14 p.

50. Shigo, A. L. and H. Marx. 1977. CODIT (Compartmentalization of decay in trees). Agric. Inf. Bull. 405. 73 p.

51. Shigo, A. L. and R. Campana. 1977. Discolored and decayed wood associated with injection wounds in American elm. J. Arboric. 3: 230-235.

52. Blanchard, R., D. Smith, A. Shigo, and L. Safford. 1978. Effects of soil applied potassium on cation distribution around wounds in red maple. Can: J. For. Res. 8: 228-231.

53. Shortle, W. C., A. L. Shigo, and J. Ochrymowych. 1978. Patterns of resistance to a pulsed electric current in sound and decayed utility poles. For. Prod. Jrnl. 28: 48-51.

54. Walters, R. and A. L. Shigo. 1978. Discoloration and decay associated with paraformaldehyde treated tapholes in sugar maple. Can. J. For. Res. 8: 54-60.

55. Shortle, W. C. and A. L. Shigo. 1978. Effect of plastic wrap on wound closure and internal compartmentalization of discolored and decayed wood in red maple. Plant Disease Reporter. 62: 999-1002.

56. Walters, R. S., and A. L. Shigo. 1978. Tapholes in sugar maples. What happens in a tree. For. Serv. Gen. Tech. Rept. NE-47. 12 p. illus.

57. Shigo, A. L., A. E. McGinnes, D. Funk, and N. Rogers. 1979. Internal defects associated with pruned and nonpruned branch stubs in black walnut. For. Serv. Res. Pap. NE-440. 27 p.

58. Mulhern, J., W. Shortle, and A. L. Shigo. 1979. Barrier zones in red maple: An optical and scanning microscope examination. For. Sci. 25: 311-316.

59. Shigo, A. L. 1979. Decay resistant trees. Proc. of the 26th Northeastern Tree Improvement Conf. 64-72.

60. Eckstein, D., W. Liese, and A. L. Shigo. 1979. Relationship of wood structure to compartmentalization of discolored wood in hybrid poplar. Can. J. For. Res. 9: 205-210.

61. Davis, W., A. L. Shigo, and R. Weyrick. 1979. Seasonal changes in electrical resistance of inner bark in red oak, red maple, and eastern white pine. For. Sci. 25: 282-286.

62. Shigo, A. L. and Walter C. Shortle. 1979. Compartmentalization of discolored wood in heartwood of red oak. Phytopathology 69: 710-711

63. Shigo, A. L. 1979. Compartmentalization of decay associated with Heterobasidion annosum in roots of Pinus resinosa. Eur. J. For. Pathol. 9: 341-347.

64. Merrill, W. and A. L. Shigo. 1979. An expanded concept of tree decay. Phytopathology 69 1158-1161.

65. Tippett, J. and A. L. Shigo. 1980. Barrier zone anatomy in red pine roots invaded by Heterobasidion annosum. Can. J. For. Res. 10: 224-232.

66. Shigo, A. L., R. Campana, F. Hyland, and J. Andersen. 1980. Anatomy of injected elms to control Dutch elm disease. J. Arboric. 6: 96-100.

67. Hawksworth, F. and A. L. Shigo. 1980. Dwarf mistletoe on red spruce in the White Mountains of New Hampshire. Plant Disease Reporter. 64: 880-882.

68. Bauch, J., A. L. Shigo, and M. Starck. 1980. Wound effects in the xylem of Acer and Betula species. Holzforschung 34: 153-160.

69. Davis, W., W. C. Shortle, and A. L. Shigo. 1980. A potential hazard rating system for fir stands infested with budworm using cambial electrical resistance. Can. J. For. Res. 10: 541-544.

70. Shigo, A. L. 1981. Proper pruning of tree branches. In: The Garden. Vol. 106: 471-473.

71. Tippett, J. T. and A. L. Shigo. 1981. Barriers to decay in conifer roots. Eur. J. For. Pathol. 11: 51-59.

72. Green, D., W. C. Shortle, and A. L. Shigo. 1981. Compartmentalization of discolored and decayed wood in red maple branch stubs. For. Sci. 27: 519-522.

73. Armstrong, J. E., A. L. Shigo, D. T. Funk, E. A. McGinnes, and D. E. Smith. 1981. A macroscopic and microscopic study of compartmentalization and wound closure after mechanical wounding of black walnut trees. Wood and Fiber 13: 275-291.

74. Shigo, A. L. and J. T. Tippett. 1981. Compartmentalization of decayed wood associated with Armillaria mellea in several tree species. For. Serv. Res. Pap. NE-488. 20 p.

75. Ostrofsky, A. and A. L. Shigo. 1981. A myxomycete isolated from discolored wood of living red maple. Mycologia 73: 997-1000.

76. Butin, H. and A. L. Shigo. 1981. Radial shakes and "frost cracks" in living oak trees. For. Serv. Res. Pap. NE-478. 21 p.

77. Tippett, J. T. and A. L. Shigo. 1981. Barrier zone formation: A mechanism of tree defense against vascular pathogens. IAWA Bull. Vol.2: 163-168.

78. Shigo, A. L. 1982. Tree health. J. Arboric. 8: 311-316.

79. Shigo, A. L. 1980. Trees resistant to spread of decay associated with wounds. In: Proc. of Third International Workshop on the Genetics of Host Parasite Interactions in Forestry; Wageningen, The Netherlands. September 14-21, 1980.

80. Shigo, A. L. 1982. Tree decay in our urban forests: What can be done about it? Plant Disease 66: 763-768.

81. Shigo, A. L. and C. L. Wilson. 1982. Wounds in peach trees. Plant Disease 66: 895-897.

82. Tippett, J. T., A. L. Bogle, and A. L. Shigo. 1983. Response to balsam fir and hemlock roots to injuries. Eur. J. For. Pathol. 2: 357-364.

83. Shigo, A. L. and W. C. Shortle. 1983. Wound dressings: Results of studies over 13 years. J. Arboric. 9: 317-329.

84. Shigo, A. L. and K. Roy. 1983. Violin woods: A new look. University of New Hampshire, Durham, NH. 67 p.

85. Shigo, A. L. 1983. Tree defects: A photo guide. USDA For. Service Gen. Tech. Report. NE-82. 167 p.

86. Shigo, A. L. 1984. Tree decay and pruning. Arboric. Jrnl. 8: 1-12.

87. Rademacher, P., J. Bauch, and A. L. Shigo. 1984. Characteristics of xylem formed after wounding in Acer, Betula, and Fagus. IAWA Bull. n.s. 5(2): 141-151.

88. Ostrofsky, A. and A. L. Shigo. 1984. Relationship between canker size and wood starch in American chestnut. Eur. J. For. Pathol. 14: 65-68.

89. Shigo, A. L. 1984. Compartmentalization: A conceptual framework for understanding how trees grow and defend themselves. Ann. Rev. Phytopathology 22: 189-214.

90. Shigo, A. L. 1984. How to assess the defect status of a stand. Northern Journal of Applied Forestry 1(3): 41-49.

91. Peters, M., P. Ossenbruggen, and A. L. Shigo. 1984. Cracking and failure behavior models of defective balsam fir trees. Holzforschung 39: 125-135.

92. Shigo, A. L. 1984. Tree defects: Cluster effect. Northern Journal of Applied Forestry 1(3): 41-49.

93. DeGraaf, R. M. and A. L. Shigo. 1985. Managing cavity trees for wildlife in the Northeast. USDA For. Serv. Gen. Tech. Rep. NE-101. 21 p.

94. Ossenbruggen, P. J., M. Peters, and A. L. Shigo. 1985. Potential failure of a decayed tree under wind loading. Wood and Fiber 18 (1): 39-48.

95. Shigo, A. L. 1985. Compartmentalization of decay in trees. Scientific American 252(4): 96-103.

96. Shigo, A. L. 1985. How tree branches are attached to trunks. Can. J. Bot. 63: 1391-1401.

97. Shigo, A. L. and K. R. Dudzik. 1985. Response of uninjured cambium to xylem injury. Wood Science and Technology 19: 6 p.

98. Shigo, A. L. and Walter C. Shortle. 1985. Shigometry — A Reference Guide. USDA, For. Serv. Agric. Handbook No. 646, 48 p.

99. Shigo, A. L. 1985. Wounded forests, starving trees. J. Forestry 83: 668-673.

100. Shigo, A. L. 1986. Journey to the center of a tree. American Forests 92: 18-22, 46-47.

101. Shigo, A., G. F. Gregory, R. J. Campana, K. R. Dudzik, and D. M. Zimel. 1986. Patterns of starch reserves in healthy and diseased American elms. Can. J. For. Res. 16: 204-210.

For a list of publications by others that were very important in developing the concepts, see the literature cited in publications 8, 11, 12, 15, 26, 89, and 96.

INDEX

Act of God 93
Adventitious buds 133, 134
Almost-closed wounds 66
Angle of cut 25, 31
Architecture 17, 145
Associates 140
Attachments, branch 18, 19

Barrier zone 141, 164, 170
BBR 26, 27, 28
Beauty 3
Big trees 12, 73, 82, 98, 103, 119, 122, 123, 135
Biomass 133
Boundaries 23, 54, 55, 60, 67, 71, 141, 154, 164
Bracing 73, 117
Branch 18, 35, 151
  attachment 18, 20
  diagram 18, 19, 151
  bark ridge 26, 27, 88
  failures 79, 80, 103, 125, 165
  protection zone 22, 40
Bonsai 136, 143, 146, 166
Buds 112, 113
Buying trees 72, 78, 88
Callus-Woundwood 15, 32, 33, 63, 69, 147, 150, 162, 164
  healing 63
  oval 34
  patterns 33
  rings 32
Cambial zone 85, 134, 164
Cankers 11, 17, 48
  Cytospora 47, 48
  Nectria 47
Care, proper 5
Cavity 55, 65, 102, 129, 131, 135, 167
  boundaries 55, 65
Cells 6, 22, 141, 144
Cell Wall 6
Cellulose and lignin 6, 141
Changes 8
Cherry 41, 57
Citrus 115
City trees 5, 8, 17, 79, 88, 91, 123, 131, 138
Cluster, branches 80
Codominant stems 70-78, 88, 91, 156, 158-161
Collars 10, 18, 20, 24, 25, 28, 35, 138, 149, 151, 157
  flat 30
  swollen 11
Compartmentalization 22, 64, 67, 138, 141, 170
Conifers 22, 30, 38, 85
Construction injury 7, 132
Coppice growth 133
Coral tree 64
Core, branch 23, 38
  colored 37, 96
Corrective pruning 17, 89, 90
Cracks 17, 36, 45, 68, 73, 99, 125, 165

Crimes 98
Cull 92
Dead branch 50, 52-54, 56, 57, 62, 77, 110, 135
Dead spots 44, 85, 113
Defects 79
Defense 6, 10, 71, 139, 141-143
  systems 2, 10, 22, 40, 47, 61, 76, 124
  limits 7, 41, 47
Destroy 3, 40, 124
Dignity 2, 91, 92, 137
Discolored wood 56, 57, 96
Dormant buds 121, 133, 134
Drill holes 55, 87, 167
Drought 46
Dutch elm disease 71, 158-161, 180

Elements, essential 19
Elite sprouts 121
Energy reserves 6, 23, 41, 49, 141, 144
Epicormic buds 134
Espalier 94, 111, 115, 143

Fertilize 118, 174, 177, 178
Flat-top cut 97
Flush cuts 10, 17, 40-49, 65, 68, 125, 136
Food 11, 19, 60, 62
Forest tree 4, 138, 146, 163
Forked stem 70
Form 83
  good 83, 88, 89, 91
  poor 17, 83, 89, 93
Framework 5, 13, 14, 17, 106, 109, 111, 112, 114, 115, 126, 127
Frost 44, 46
  cracks 45
Fruit bodies, fungi 34, 64, 103, 131
Future 138

Grapevines 105, 114
Grass 116

Hardwoods 22, 39
Hazard trees 12, 13, 36, 74, 81, 82, 91, 93, 98, 99, 101, 122-125, 131, 172, 173
Healing 63, 64, 67, 141, 147, 150
Health 60, 145
Heartrot 56
Heartwood 56, 142
Heat 44-46, 121
Hollows 87
Hypoxylon 47

Included bark 17, 78-87, 134, 162, 163
Infections 15, 40, 54, 64, 71
Insects 43, 62

Lightning 99

Microorganisms 62, 130, 161
Mutilation 108, 147
Myths, wound dressings 63, 128

Natural shedding 21, 28, 29, 62
Natural target pruning 28, 29, 37

Oils 22
Orchards 115, 146
Over pruning 7, 13, 120, 121

Pathogen   20, 54, 56, 60, 71, 100
Perch sites   135
People   5, 67, 88, 89, 139, 141, 180
Phenols   22
Photosynthate   19
Pleaching   94
Planting   116, 118, 174, 175
Pollard   14, 94, 104, 109, 126, 143
  head   14, 105, 107, 114, 127, 133
  improper   14
Power lines   12, 17, 88, 101, 107, 123, 125
Problems   8, 9-15, 36, 68
Protection zone   22, 38, 40, 54, 62, 63,
                        138, 148, 150, 154
Pruning
  best time   31
  improper   3, 33-36, 38, 39, 96
  proper   2, 17, 25, 26, 28, 30,
               32, 37, 38, 39, 62, 76, 86, 87

Reaction zone   141, 164, 170
Reserve energy   101
Respect   2, 141
Roots   13, 47, 100, 118, 132
Rots   11, 22, 34, 39, 47, 51, 55, 58, 59,
                          60, 69, 129

Safety first   16, 135
Sap flow   31
Sapwood   6, 42, 56
Starch   22
Stubs   11, 25, 27, 61, 62, 76, 109
Sugar   19
Support, mechanical   23
Suppressed sprouts   121
Scribing   51, 130
Shaping   110
Shearing   113
Shedding   29, 144, 166
Size and shape   126, 127, 136, 138, 146

Snag, wildlife   135
Site   9, 17, 116
Specimen tree   88
Spikes, climbing   43, 130
Sprouts   14, 49, 101, 102, 124
  excessive   13, 49, 101, 121, 123
Stem bark ridge   70, 72, 76, 88
Stump sprouts   133
Sterilize, wounds   65
Strapping   117
Sunken spots   17, 47, 72

Terpenes   22
Tipping   12, 90, 94, 120, 122-124
Timber   17
Training cuts   94-98
Transport, liquids   6, 23
Tree   5, 17, 35, 137, 141-143

Vines   114

Waste, money   89, 93, 131
Water   19, 55, 87, 116
Weak unions   72, 75, 78, 91, 92, 102, 133
Weakness, signs   40, 41, 43, 47, 73
Wildlife   129, 135
Wire in hose   117
Wisterias   105, 114
Wood   5, 6
Wound   17, 34, 36, 67, 165
Wound dressings   7, 15, 17, 63, 65, 68,
                       128-131, 137, 150
Woundwood   15, 32, 33, 63-69, 147, 152,
                          153, 162, 164

Yews   113
Young tree training   12, 73, 87, 88, 89, 94,
                       103, 109, 111, 112

Zones   22, 27

And the Lord God took the man,
and put him into the garden of Eden
to dress it and to keep it.

Genesis 2:15

STILL OUR RESPONSIBILITY!

TREE PRUNING

has been published in a first edition of ten thousand copies.
Designed by Dr. Alex L. Shigo assisted by Everett Rowley,
composition in Garamond and printing were executed by
Sherwin/Dodge Printers in Littleton, New Hampshire,
the text on Shorewood Gloss, the cover on Kivar 9.
Binding was by New Hampshire Bindery
in Concord, New Hampshire.

Back Cover:
Koalas have been pruning trees for millions of years.
Koalas depend on healthy trees for their survival.
Humans and many other living things depend on healthy trees for their survival.
Let us not forget what is said in Genesis 2:15, and what the fox told the Little Prince.

TOUCH TREES